CONTENTS

TABLES

INDEPENDENT STUDY

Two examples from English higher education

Keith Percy & Paul Ramsden
with John Lewin

Society for Research into Higher Education

SB 14813 [5.25 . 11.80

Research into Higher Education Monographs

The Society for Research into Higher Education, University of Surrey, Guildford, Surrey GU2 5XH

First published 1980

ISBN 0 900868 75 9

Printed in England by Stephen Austin and Sons Ltd, Hertford

ACKNOWLEDGEMENTS

We are grateful to the many people who have helped us in producing this book: the students and staff at Lancaster University and North East London Polytechnic who co-operated in the evaluatory studies; John Lewin for his collaboration in the preparation of Chapter 3; Jane Routh, Bill Fuge, Duncan Nimmo, Vernon Pratt and Brian Wynne of Lancaster, and John Stephenson, Simon Gray and Derek Robbins of NELP, for their many helpful comments on an earlier draft of the manuscript. Except where we have expressly stated otherwise, the opinions stated in the book concerning both independent study schemes are ours alone.

Keith Percy
Paul Ramsden
Lancaster, April 1979

Since 1972 two comprehensive schemes of independent study have been introduced into undergraduate education in the United Kingdom. One programme is at Lancaster University and the other is at North East London Polytechnic (NELP). This monograph brings together reports on both of them.

The development and practice of the two programmes has excited considerable interest. The reasons are not hard to find. Among them are the evidence of student dissatisfaction with conventional courses, criticisms by employers and the government that higher education is irrelevant to subsequent employment, and the desire of colleges outside the university system of higher education to grasp new ideas and new roles in order to secure their institutional future. The real concerns of all universities, colleges and polytechnics to make themselves attractive to a shrinking pool of potential future applicants are also pressing. Clearly the extent to which the NELP and Lancaster independent study schemes have broken new ground successfully, and have produced an efficient and relevant mode of undergraduate education which encourages both student learning and student satisfaction, is a matter of urgent concern for the rest of higher education.

Chapter 1 of this book sets the scene for the case studies which form the main part of the monograph. In it, we examine several notions of independence in learning and discuss the background against which programmes of independent study in British higher education have been evolved. We have not attempted here to review the history and practice of independent study in American colleges, but for an introduction to this area a reader might turn to Dressel and Thompson's recent work (Dressel and Thompson 1973).

Chapters 2 and 3 present the case studies of the Lancaster and NELP independent studies schemes. We know that the case studies have their limitations. As small-scale evaluatory pieces of research they were carried out in their local situation without reference to, or knowledge of each other, and were only brought together when completed. In some ways they are not fully comparable. Nevertheless, they provide important evidence on the issues associated with the operation of independent studies schemes and on the obstacles to their success. The fieldwork at NELP was carried out by Paul Ramsden in 1975/76. The fieldwork at Lancaster was carried out by John Lewin in 1976. Some initial interviewing of students at Lancaster was undertaken by Duncan Nimmo in 1975.

In Chapter 4 we summarize developments at NELP and Lancaster since the evaluatory studies. We also look at the differences between the schemes and discuss the common issues that arise from the two experiences. What are the successes and failures of independent study schemes? What developments and improvements are desirable, and what implications are indicated for higher education in the 1980s?

We feel it is right that the last word on the two schemes should be left to those presently responsible for them. The book therefore concludes with postscripts from John Stephenson of North East London Polytechnic and from Jane Routh of Lancaster University.

'INDEPENDENCE IN LEARNING'

Over 120 years ago, Cardinal Newman argued that 'self-education in any shape, in the most restricted sense, is preferable to a system of teaching which, professing so much, really does so little for the mind.' Newman went on to claim that those students 'who dispense with the stimulus and support of instructors' are more likely:

> 'to have more thought, more mind, more philosophy, more true enlargement, than those earnest but ill-used persons who are forced to load their minds with a score of subjects against an examination, who have too much on their hands to indulge themselves in thinking or investigation, who devour premiss and conclusion together with indiscriminate greediness, who hold whole sciences on faith, and commit demonstrations to memory, and who too often, as might be expected, when their period of education is passed, throw up all they have learned in disgust, having gained nothing really by their anxious labours, except perhaps the habit of application.'

(Newman 1852)

Newman's eloquent critique came long before the development of most of the features which are commonplace in the British student's experience of higher education in the 1970s: universities and colleges of several thousand students, large lecture groups, non-residential education, course work assessment, an acknowledged role for universities and colleges in the production of highly qualified personnel for subsequent employment, and the right of students to a grant-aided place in higher education once the minimum entry qualification has been secured. Each of these characteristics has its positive aspects and is related to the extension of educational opportunities to a larger proportion of the population, to a more equitable assessment of higher education performance and to the appropriate employment of the talents and intelligence which earn a degree. But there are those who would argue that these developments have had deleterious effects on the quality of education available to students. It might be said that Newman's preference for 'self-education' over some contemporary 'systems of teaching' is more appropriate today than it was in Newman's own time.

British higher education is now a heterogeneous system: methods of teaching vary, and many different kinds of courses are offered in very different institutions. It may seem unwise, therefore, to generalize about the difficulties its students and teachers face. But recent research findings provide some prima facie justification for a general concern about the educational value of many students' experiences of higher education. In the early 1970s researchers from Lancaster University carried out a large-scale survey of staff and student opinions at a number of universities, polytechnics and colleges. Staff who were interviewed shared uniform beliefs that the majority of their students did not work as hard, or as effectively, as could be wished: the educational benefit they derived from their courses was partial, their experience of learning was superficial; the general staff view appeared to be that:

> 'there were a few good students—students able to enter into the subject, make it their own and evaluate it critically; but many "bad", weak, mediocre or average students of different kinds.'

(Entwistle and Percy 1974)

Another aspect of the same research investigated student reports of their educational experience over a wide range of vocational and non-vocational courses at universities and polytechnics. Without prompting, students frequently picked as the most beneficial aspects of their academic experience work in which they had freedom to make decisions about course content and methods of learning. Most students wanted challenge and stimulus from their courses; they were most likely to find it when freed from constraints of syllabus and course structure in, for example, self-directed project work:

> 'It seems very clear from our research that students in all fields of study believe that they would learn more, and enjoy learning more, if they had greater control over the pace of their learning, more chance to determine the subject matter of their courses and were less rigidly inhibited by traditional conceptions of disciplinary boundaries and what constitutes the proper study of a particular subject. Students very often made comments describing the "most satisfying aspect" of their course as "the work which I have been allowed to do myself" and were highly critical of a curriculum structure which imposed a logic and sequence of learning on them which they felt was less educational and less motivating than one suggested to them by their own developing intellectual interests.'

(Brennan and Percy 1977)

Between 1972 and 1974, coincident with the Lancaster research, members of the Nuffield Foundation's Group for Research and Innovation in Higher Education made a series of visits to universities and reported that they were 'introduced to many schemes purporting to provide greater independence for the learner'. There were, they observed, 'diverse recent innovations concerned with a less teacher-dependent way of learning at the undergraduate level' (Nuffield Group 1975). In fact, the Nuffield Group publications reveal the great variety of pedagogic practice which they chose to put together under the label 'independence in learning'. The recent innovations ranged from the Lancaster School of Independent Studies—in which students could be seen to be negotiating the goals and content of their studies and the nature of their assessment—to examples of programmed learning, of study schemes based on the Keller Plan, of individual and group projects, and of laboratory work.

The NELP and Lancaster schemes of independent study were thus not, it would seem, generated in isolation from other movements within higher education during the early 1970s. There is some evidence of widespread student support of increased independence in learning and of attempts by institutions of higher education to provide it.[1] Before we begin to examine the NELP and Lancaster experiences, it may be helpful if we try to make clearer the variety of meanings which underlie the broad-based notion of 'independence in learning'.

'INDIVIDUALIZED' AND 'INDEPENDENT' STUDY

It seems fruitful to draw a distinction between 'individualized' and 'independent' study. Many of the innovations observed by the Nuffield Group were concerned with a particular methodology of learning prescribed areas of knowledge or pre-determined skills. The 'independence' involved was conceived as a means of promoting student motivation, of adjusting the pace of academic work to take account of student differences and of developing better specific problem-solving techniques. In real senses the students were not independent of their teachers at all. A teacher does not have to be physically present for learning to be teacher-dependent. Project work, distance learning, resource-based learning, Keller Plan, programmed learning, essay writing, seminar preparation, background reading: all of these may or may not incorporate elements of student control over learning, but by no means do they imply independence. Teaching machines—to take an extreme example—allow individual learning but provide a highly controlled dependent learning environment. Project work may be individualized but require dependence on teacher direction. So-called independent reading may be of prescribed texts. The fact that reading is carried out in the students' own time—or selectively avoided—implies only a small amount of independence of the teacher. Open University courses typically provide for a great deal of individual study, but the constraints of the learning materials, content, and assessment methods allow little independence beyond a degree of self-pacing. The collection of reports of schemes of individual learning in undergraduate science, edited by Bridge and Elton (1977), ranges widely over the varieties of self-paced and teacher-paced individual study that are possible, and over the use of individual study in laboratory work or as 'optional supplementary material' to lecture and media-based courses.

Talk of student 'independence' needs to begin from the question: of what is the student to be independent? In theory, at least, he might be independent of teachers, of fellow students, of prescribed course content or methods of learning, of specialisms and publicly acknowledged categorizations of knowledge, of limitations on sequence or pace of learning, of assessment, even of academic conventions in the use of evidence and sources. When a student simply works on his own on indi-vidually set tasks, when he has some control over the pace or mode of learning, or some choice between options, it may be more realistic to talk of 'individualized'

6

study. A possible conceptualization of the relationship between individualized and 'independent' study and of degrees of student independence (based on Boud and Bridge 1974) marks out four linked stages of student independence:

1 PACE Student can work at his own pace and choose the times (and sometimes the places) at which he finds it most appropriate to learn. Examples: Keller Plan courses; parts of many traditionally organized university courses (eg essay writing and individual reading); some project and laboratory work.

2 CHOICE Student chooses to work or not to work at a course, or at a part of a course. Examples: Keller Plan (to a limited extent); choice between a number of courses offered by a department during an academic year; modular course structures; choice of major and minor options.

3 METHOD Student can decide the method of learning he finds most suitable. Examples: independent study programmes; parts of some traditionally organized courses and individualized packages (eg choice between video presentations or texts; choice between different textbooks).

4 CONTENT Student chooses what he wants to learn according to his own goals and interests. This may or may not imply working within established academic disciplines or structures. Examples: some project work; independent study programmes.

The notion of student control over content and method in this scheme necessarily subsumes that of control over pace and choice.

The American writers Dressel and Thompson (1973) also emphasize the distinction between 'individualized' and 'independent' study. Their book—significantly entitled 'a *new* interpretation of concepts, practices and problems'—defines independent study as 'the student's self-directed pursuit of academic competence in as autonomous a manner as he is able to exercise at any particular time.' They are concerned to delineate a concept of independent study which is not seen as confined to able students alone. In contrast, many of the American schemes they survey are solely the province of a small group of highly competent students.[2] Dressel and Thompson do not allow that independent study, properly conceived, can be superimposed on rigidly established course patterns. Higher education, they imply, is primarily concerned with 'academic competence'. The particular notions of self-directed and autonomous study are intrinsic to the larger concept of 'academic competence'. Independent study is 'a capability to be developed' and 'comes close to being if it is not, indeed, the major goal of all education'.

Individualization of learning tasks, observe Dressel and Thompson, can be the 'first step toward independence' but if it is 'always accompanied by detailed task specification it may actually deny an individual even the degree of independence implicit in the anonymity of the traditional class'. Individualization may foster the motivation for independent work and, if properly conducted, will merge into independent study as responsibility for direction is transferred from teacher to student. But independent and individualized study are not equivalent. They may or may not be associated together. In a scheme of independent study it would be conceivable that a student would at different times be working alone, in a group of others, or in a dependent relationship with a teacher. The choice would relate to the goals of the particular scheme of study. This is a point that the Nuffield Group also make when they introduce the concept of 'autonomy' as signifying the ability of the student 'to choose between dependence and independence as he perceives the need' (Nuffield Group 1975).

INDEPENDENT STUDY AND 'SELF-KNOWLEDGE' AS GOALS OF HIGHER EDUCATION

Several important points emerge from Dressel and Thompson's discussion. Essentially they argue that independent study is intrinsic to the notion of a higher education. A student cannot claim to have been educated successfully at university or college unless he has learned to study independently. He will be able to exercise responsible choice over what and how to study. What also seem to be implied are the motivation and commitment to make those choices, the curiosity of the self-motivating learner who desires to find out and has an awareness of what might be found out. Acquisition of particular stocks of knowledge or defined skills are not inherent in the idea of a higher education; particular knowledge or skills can be forgotten or become outdated. But it may be argued that the commitment to pursue new knowledge and skills, and the ability to do so when tutorial guidance is no longer easily available, are, as Dressel and Thompson call them, 'the major goal of education'. Most of the British higher education staff interviewed in the Lancaster research would have accepted such a view (Entwistle and Percy 1971, 1974).

It is significant that Dressel and Thompson confine their discussion of independent study to the realms of 'academic competence'. There are others who would want to relate notions of student control over methods of learning and course content to more extended ideas of 'life competence'. A British vice-chancellor, writing of the foundation of one of the new universities, urged that:

> 'in gaining mastery over an area of enquiry (students) have gained in the process mastery over self, have discovered what it is to be self-moving, self-driven, autonomous agents, rather than to be merely responsive to pressures from outside'.

> (Fulton 1966)

Chapters 2 and 3 of this book reveal clearly how, among some of the protagonists of the Lancaster and NELP schemes of independent study, concern for the process of intellectual development fused with a determination to allow students the opportunity of setting foot on the path towards self-knowledge. Ideas of this kind are set out with some force in the works of humanistic psychologists such as Carl Rogers and Abraham Maslow. The prescriptions of Rogers, for example, have been generated from the experience of client-orientated therapy in which the psychiatrist abandoned a directive role. In his key book on education—appropriately entitled

Freedom to Learn (Rogers 1969)—Rogers, in a parallel fashion, diminishes the directive roles of tutor and teacher. He begins with the premises that 'human beings have a natural potentiality for learning' and that 'significant learning takes place when the subject matter is perceived by the student as having relevance for his own purposes'. The contrast to be made at all levels of education is between 'participative' and 'passive' learning. When a student:

'chooses his own directions, helps to discover his own learning resources, formulates his own problems, decides his own course of action, lives with the consequences of each of these choices, then significant learning is maximised.'

Rogers' philosophy of education, as many have commented, is a disarmingly 'pure' one, setting aside worldly pressures of finance and future employment, of assessment and certification. In a similar vein, Maslow (1973) argues that in an ideal college, there would be no certification, 'no credits, no degrees and no required courses. A person would be free to learn what he wanted to learn'. The point of higher education is to find oneself. The chief goals should be 'the discovery of identity' and the 'discovery of vocation'—

'What do we mean by the discovery of identity? We mean finding out what your real desires and characteristics are, and being able to live in a way that expresses them. You learn to be authentic, to be honest in the sense of allowing your behaviour and your speed to be the true and spontaneous expression of your inner feelings.'

In a college career, the student must be set on the road to 'self-actualisation'.

Such educational ideals have to be placed in the context of the practicalities of current higher education provision and must be interpreted in the light of what we know about students from research into their academic attitudes and abilities. Key questions for schemes of independent study in higher education, however defined, are to what extent students are able to exercise 'freedom to learn' from the very beginning and whether models of client-orientated therapy are the appropriate ones for tutorial guidance. There is sufficient evidence of student differences in goals, study habits and learning styles, as well as—of course—in ability, personality and attitude (see, for example, the research and literature surveys in Entwistle and Wilson 1977) to support the argument that students will vary in their initial ability to study independently and in their motivation to do so. To be able to exercise choice over content and learning method may then be a quality which, as Dressel and Thompson suggest, has to be developed over time and through a variety of individualized and independent learning situations. The issue of whether the freedom given to students in schemes of independent study should be immediate or developmental is hedged around by some complicated value judgements and difficult pedagogic decisions.

What follows is an attempt to describe the origins, form, and development of two schemes of independent study and, particularly through the eyes of early participants in the schemes, we will try to make some estimate of the problems and possibilities of independent study, whether defined in terms of 'academic competence' or 'self actualization'. The following chapters are also, inevitably, a contribution to the study of the politics of innovation in British higher education and serve to illustrate the issues—relating to individuals and institutions—that confront those who would seek to translate educational ideals into educational practice.

NOTES

[1] Indeed, Adderley et al. (1975) suggest that the project method, whether called that or not, has a history in British undergraduate teaching, particularly in science courses, that reaches back into the 1920s.

[2] It is beyond the scope of this book to review the history of independent study in American higher education. Dressel and Thompson take the view that, despite the large number of so-called independent study programmes developed since the 1920s in the United States, there were few which measured up to their definition. There is a large literature on the topic: see, for example, Aydelotte (1924), Umstattd (1935), Aydelotte (1944), Bonthius et al. (1957), Brick and McGrath (1969), Dressel and DeLisle (1969).

ORIGINS AND BACKGROUND

In 1972 the James Committee (James 1972) presented the findings of its inquiry into the education and training of teachers. One of its recommendations was that two-year courses of higher education, equivalent in standard to the first two years of an undergraduate degree, should be established. These courses would meet what the Committee perceived as a national need for more flexibly trained manpower; they would not be of a specialist or narrowly vocational nature. They would lead to the award of a Diploma of Higher Education. The Government accepted these proposals (DES 1972) but widened the remit of the new qualification. It would not necessarily be associated with programmes of teacher education and was to be acceptable both as a qualification in its own right—as entry to employment—and as a foundation for further study. The DipHE was to provide a general education, but it would include a specialist component. It would be validated by existing degree-awarding bodies and minimum entry requirements were to be the same as for degree courses. Mandatory local authority grants would be available to students.

The origins of the DipHE at North East London Polytechnic lay in a decision made by Dr. G. S. Brosan, the polytechnic's director, to establish a working party to plan a course which would lead to the award of the new diploma. This initiative was taken, and the working party began its deliberations, even before the Government had officially approved the James proposals. By late 1972 the working party had drawn up proposals for a DipHE which followed the James recommendations but used them as a means of creating a radically different sort of higher education course. The James Report had suggested that DipHE courses should incorporate flexible course structures and teaching methods; whether its authors expected that this would lead to a propqsal as far reaching as that from NELP is not recorded.

Among the thirty polytechnics NELP has been conspicuous in its attempts to articulate a distinct 'polytechnic philosophy'. It has been at pains to emphasize that, while its role is distinct from that of the universities, it shares common interests with the further education system. The development of the NELP ideology was due in no small part to the innovatory zeal of George Brosan. He came to NELP with a history of innovations behind him, particularly as the principal of Enfield College of Technology. He went out of his way to attract an intelligent and lively staff to the polytechnic, including two eloquent spokesmen of the policy that future expansion in higher education should take place outside the universities (the 'binary policy'): Eric Robinson and Tyrrell Burgess.

Brosan observed that the fact 'that polytechnics exist at all is . . . the result of a correspondingly remarkable social failure of universities' (Brosan 1971a). Robinson and Burgess have been bitterly critical in their publications of the élitist, closed nature of university higher education. Underpinning the NELP educational ideology is a belief that the universities have failed to meet the needs of a large group of prospective students, particularly local and working-class students. Burgess (1977) has argued, moreover, against what he sees to be the universities' over-emphasis on the inherently conservative demands of the academic disciplines. It amounts, he maintains, to a devaluation in the students' status as a learner. Robinson asserts:

> 'Sooner or later this country must face a comprehensive reform of education beyond school—a reform which will bring higher education out of the ivory towers and make it available for all.'
>
> (Robinson 1968)

According to these arguments, it is futile to try to tackle the problem of unequal access to higher education through the university system. The solution lies in developing different kinds of institutions. The model for these institutions is the traditional working-class means of social mobility: the further education system. Burgess has described this as the 'service' tradition of post-school education, and has characterized it as open, innovatory, and vocational.

Under the direction of George Brosan, NELP has consistently repudiated an image of itself as primarily responsible to the academic community represented by the universities. Its prospectuses and publicity documents emphasize the polytechnic's commitment to serve the 'needs' of the local community. Its courses should be 'relevant' and should seek to encourage vocational competence; they should, ideally, be open to all those prospective students who are 'likely to benefit' from them, and not be restricted to entrants who possess certain formal entry requirements. The DipHE working party consisted of seven members of the polytechnic's staff; it included both Burgess and Robinson. Clearly, it immediately defined its role as the development of a course appropriate to a 'service' concept of higher education and to the NELP 'philosophy'.

It seems that the notion of independent study grew more or less logically from the premises which the DipHE working party set itself. The working party began the planning of the course using a basic systems approach; the problem they considered was defined in terms of the students whom they thought were likely to enter the course and the capacities they wished them to achieve at the end of it. A range of general skills ('competences')—such as the ability to formulate and test problems and to identify relevant sources of information—was outlined. The needs of students were important, the needs and boundaries of academic disciplines unimportant. The working party, and the development group which subsequently produced the DipHE submission to the CNAA, gradually moved into a position in which it felt that these aims could best be achieved by a programme of independent study. What could be less like traditional higher education, or more in line with the needs of students—especially those who had not hitherto demanded higher education?

It was envisaged that the proposed programme of studies would fulfil the needs of several groups of prospective students who wished to continue their formal education but who were not attracted to either a specific vocational course or to the study of a particular academic discipline. These students might include school-leavers without a commitment to a particular sixth-form subject, mature students who had worked for several years and wished to return to education before deciding on a career, and those who were already established in a career but wanted to move to a different one. In the proposed scheme, responsibility for planning a programme of study, for choosing specific objectives, and for deciding on the means by which their achievement would be tested, was devolved to the student. There would be no syllabus or course content in the usual sense; no formal lecture programmes; no set assignments which all students completed: even the arrangements for teaching would 'remain tentative pending student participation in their development' (NELP 1973). A modular course structure, which other colleges implementing DipHE programmes were to evolve, was rejected.[2]

The method of course organization adopted at NELP for the DipHE was overtly based upon a theory of education derived from the work of Karl Popper (Popper 1959; Burgess 1977). On this view, all learning takes place through a process of formulating problems, solving them and testing the solutions. The act of participating in this process is valuable in itself, for it promotes an autonomous frame of mind, even if the formulations and solutions are not new. A student who sets his own objectives and proposes solutions to them will become an independent learner.[3] For Burgess, as for Popper, a political philosophy of liberalism underlies this position: 'progress' in an open society is the product of the rigorous testing of received opinions and values. But there were other, less openly acknowledged influences on the NELP DipHE. The ideas and experiences reported by Dressel and Thompson (1973) would seem to have shaped the form of the course, particularly with regard to the use of group projects, the notion of independent study as the development of 'competence', and the extension of independent study to students who are not obviously 'academically superior'. There are also powerful echoes in the DipHE documentation of the ideas of John Dewey (1916), particularly the identification of a need for problem-based learning and discovery within a changing, democratic society. Each of these influences is apparent in one of the earlier DipHE prospectuses:

'We in the School (for Independent Study) hold that in our modern ever-changing society much knowledge becomes obsolete. We therefore believe that it is more important to possess the ability to adapt to a new situation and to acquire new information than it is to retain knowledge in particular subjects . . . We also believe that higher education has neglected the importance of working with people . . . a major element of our educational programmes is "group work'' in which students plan, carry out and assess their work as a team . . . The function of the School is to help people define their intellectual, social and personal needs within the context of our particular philosophy of education, and then to assist them to achieve their goals. This is done by a "problem-centred" approach to learning—that is, by encouraging students, either as a group or as individuals, to formulate problems, propose solutions and then put them into practice to test them . . . Above all, because the School is committed to the view that because competence does not depend exclusively upon accumulated knowledge, we argue that rigid insistence upon traditional entry requirements is inappropriate.'

(NELP 1975)

It would seem, then, that the NELP DipHE—like most educational innovations—was the product of a range of loosely-connected practical requirements, policies, and beliefs. Amongst the more important of these were the desires of men such as Brosan, Burgess, and Robinson, who wished to produce highly innovatory courses; the government's need for two-year programmes of higher education; the anti-élitism (some would say, anti-academicism) of the binary policy; the pragmatic approach to meeting the demands of employers and students ('needs' and 'relevance'); and the values and theories of education of Popper and Dewey. To these we might add the wishes of certain members of the working party to offer students opportunities denied to them in conventional courses for personal growth and the development of social skills, based on American ideas of group therapy, management training, and counselling. These latter ideas were not unattractive to George Brosan, who had previously experimented with group exercises in the liberal studies course at Enfield. 'We are beginning to see the end,' he observed, soon after becoming director of NELP, 'of teaching in a purely syntactical mode remote from the immediacy of sense data and personal experiences. I think that we are almost ready to embark on a re-styling of curricula which involve the elements of life that are personal, real and expressive, rather than merely intellectual' (Brosan 1971b).

The proposal for the new diploma course was strongly supported by the director and had a fairly easy passage through the decision-making structure of the polytechnic. The proposal was submitted to the CNAA in 1973 and was given limited experimental support for a period of two years. The programme began to operate in 1974 within the newly established School for Independent Study. The title of the school struck a nice (and deliberate) note of ambiguity, in its implied reference to both means and ends. The school had the status of a faculty within the polytechnic; later (in 1978) it would be merged with the Faculty of Arts to create a new Faculty of Humanities.

STRUCTURE OF THE PROGRAMME, 1974–76
Entry Requirements, Admission, and Student Progress
The CNAA had expressed much concern over the polytechnic's proposed entry

requirements, and over the proportion of 'A' level to mature and 'non-standard'[4] entrants, in the new course. The James Report recommended that entry to the DipHE should be based on two 'A' levels but with 'generous provision for exception'. The planners of the NELP programme seized on this opportunity to put into practice the flexible entry policy of the NELP 'philosophy'. They argued that entry should be dependent on the applicant's level of motivation, his understanding of the programme, and his ability to benefit from it. They wished also to give more weight to qualifications attained in further education colleges, such as Ordinary National Diplomas. Since the programme did not depend on previous performance in any academic area, they argued, conventional entry requirements could be waived. The CNAA had suggested that non-'A' level applicants ought to show 'evidence of ability' to cope with the course: for example, by writing an extended essay.

In practice, applicants were selected for admission to the course very largely on the basis of an interview. Up to twelve prospective students met a group of DipHE tutors, one of whom outlined the programme in some detail. Individual interviews then followed. In these, the tutor attempted to assess the applicant's understanding of the programme, his level of motivation, and whether he would benefit from it. Efforts were made to counsel each applicant about his possible choices; applicants were referred to other courses if it was felt that these would better meet their needs.[5] Student progress records for the first intake of 1974 are a revealing commentary on the school's entry policy and method of selection. In Table 1 (page 32) the high level of student wastage for the 1974 entry (29 per cent) is immediately apparent. It is clear that mature and non-standard entrants were more likely to withdraw than 'A' level entrants.

The level of wastage for the 1975 entry was even higher; nearly 45 per cent of all students did not enter for the final assessment. To be fair, many of the withdrawals took place after the course's planning period (see below), after which students had achieved a clearer idea of their educational needs, and many of those withdrawing found places on other courses more suited to their requirements. It is also significant that of students who literally stayed the course and entered for final assessment, mature and non-standard students were about as likely to pass as were 'A' level entrants (Table 2, page 32).

General Organization of the Programme

When the programme began in 1974, seven full-time members of academic staff (all but one of whom had been involved in planning the course during the previous year) were attached to the school. In 1975 another five joined the group. In addition, however, many more staff from other faculties of the polytechnic had a part-time commitment to the course, acting as special interest tutors to students in the school. In 1974/75 fifty-nine staff acted in this way. One lecturer from each faculty also worked as 'faculty linkman' to co-ordinate special interest studies.

The basic characteristics of the NELP independent study programme will already be apparent. In effect, the course was a device through which students created their own programmes of higher education. There was an emphasis on the acquisition of transferable skills and competences and on knowledge which was based on problems other than those defined by the disciplines. In its stress on weakened boundaries between subject areas, on supra-disciplinary concepts, and on student control over the way in which knowledge is transmitted, the programme approaches Bernstein's characterization of the 'integrated knowledge code' in education (Bernstein 1971).

The programme was organized in three main sections: planning period, central studies activities (sometimes referred to as 'group work'), and special interest studies (since renamed 'individual work'). For the first two years of the programme, the *planning period* lasted for six weeks at the beginning of the student's course. The organizers of the programme recognized that students would enter with a wide range of different qualifications and that they would be differently motivated. The planning period was designed to help students deal with the unusual task of creating a programme of studies for themselves. During this time, they were intended to come to terms with their own educational strengths and weaknesses; to improve basic competences, if necessary, in numeracy and literacy; to understand the nature and purpose of the Diploma programme; to formulate personal educational objectives and the criteria for assessing them; to have planned programmes of special interest and central studies activities to help achieve their objectives. This was—as we shall see—to prove to be an over-ambitious set of tasks for many students to tackle in six weeks. The first two of these weeks were devoted mainly to group and personal exercises designed to make clear the student's view of knowledge and to help him practise co-operation with other students. In the next two weeks, an emphasis was placed on the programme's approach to knowledge and on the elaboration of general objectives. The final part of the planning period involved the choice of special interest study and negotiation between the student and his tutor before drawing up a DipHE programme and signing of a 'contract' for it. In 1974 only very general indications of what the contract should contain were included to guide students; in 1975 a draft form of planning statement was provided in an attempt to make the requirements more explicit and less confusing.

Contracts at the end of the planning period included details of skills, knowledge and qualities that the student intended to develop by the end of the course. They revealed a variety of levels of objectives and generality of aims. Thus a student might define one objective (perhaps playing safe by reiterating a programme aim) as 'to be able to define problems as they arise, propose solutions and evaluate those solutions' and another as 'to develop layout and exhibition skills in photographic materials'. There were also considerable differences between different students' objectives. These differences between students and between the same student's objectives were to be expected; the problems arose in defining the objectives in the first place, in knowing whether they related to what tutors expected, and in relating them to the final assessment procedures.

In its submission to the CNAA for a DipHE the polytechnic recognized that allowing students to set their own objectives might lead to widely varying standards. In an attempt to guarantee the quality of students' work an external validating board was established. The board, whose members in 1974/5 included Lady Plowden, Asa Briggs, Sir Toby Weaver, and Lord James, met once in the middle of each term. After the planning period it scrutinized the statements of objectives made by students, and in certain cases discussed the statements with tutors and students; recommendations were made for revised statements of objectives and methods in some cases.

Clearly, the planning period of the course and the subsequent validation of objectives formed a crucial time in the student's experience of the NELP DipHE. It was followed by the two major parallel parts of the student's course: central studies and special interest studies. The *central studies* part of the course was, in the terms of the James Report, the broadly based general education envisaged for the DipHE student. In Dewey's conception of educational method, it approximates to his requirement for lifelike 'occupations' as learning situations. Students were required to spend up to two days a week working in groups of two to twenty members on projects which they devised themselves. Examples of these projects in 1974/5 included:

—Study of enclosed green areas in Inner London
—Individual conscience and corporate authority
—From Inverness to Fort William by canoe
—Advertising and the use of colour
—Concept-reality of commercial radio in London
—The personal reading habits of 15 year-olds

The first intake of students was divided into seminar groups of twelve and to each of these groups was attached one of the full-time lecturers in the school. This staff member acted as personal adviser to the students while also supervising their projects. During the second year of the course's operation, the procedure was varied for the new intake, so that project tutors and personal tutors need no longer be the same; the tutor group met once a week with the same tutor (their personal adviser) to discuss general problems with progress, although individual students would be members of other groups for the purposes of their group projects.

The third component of the programme, *special interest* studies, ran concurrently with the central studies activities. It relates to the 'opportunity to study in depth' mentioned by James. Students worked as individuals on projects chosen by themselves; although they were not committed to one project for the whole of their two years, in 1974 and 1975 they could normally introduce changes only at the end of the first term or at the end of the first year. During the planning period students devised, in consultation with a specialist tutor, programmes of work in the field of their individual interests. The constraints and freedoms of special interest studies for the student resembled those of a research student; he might be expected to assist his tutor in his research, to prepare teaching material, to attend parts of other polytechnic courses, to spend time outside the polytechnic on fieldwork, to carry out

surveys and experiments, and to read, think, and plan in depth in the area of his specialism. Some examples of special interest studies in 1974/5 included:
—Child development and language
—1920s fashion
—Underwater technology and marine biology
—Systems and information theory
—Libraries and their community
—Electrical engineering
—Teaching methods in Mathematics

Assessment

The submission of proposals for the NELP DipHE to the CNAA laid stress upon the assessment process as a way of providing a framework in which the student could monitor his own progress. An explicit distinction was made between this type of assessment and qualifying assessment. Monitoring assessment would be carried out by the student with the help of his tutors and peers; comments and advice would help the student to identify areas in which agreed objectives were not being met and to determine remedial action. The process by which this formative assessment would be carried out was not properly formulated before the programme began and the deficiency created many difficulties for students (see below, page 22).

Qualifying (summative) assessment, for the purposes of indicating a student's level of competence at the end of the course, was carried out by an assessment board comprising tutors, external examiners, and other polytechnic representatives. Qualifying assessment took two forms. The central studies part of the programme was assessed by observing each student in a small group in the process of tackling a given project during the final term. This amounted in effect to a term-long oral and written examination: a very demanding task. The intention was to evaluate the general competences developed in group work during the two years; put another way, the aim was to judge the extent to which the student had learned now to work collaboratively with others to solve problems. The nature of this 'set situation' examination effectively limited the range of students' specific objectives, although it was not clear in the first year just what the limits were. Students were also expected to demonstrate their ability in agreed specific skills related to their special interest work. Here, the examiners considered the product of individual work; this might take the form of a conventional report, or, as in 1976, exhibitions and models might be presented. There was considerable student choice in what materials were to be assessed; any activity which he had undertaken in the course might be used as part of the submission of work.

Post-diploma Programmes

James intended that DipHE courses should provide a qualification which would be recognized both in its own right as a terminal equivalent to the first two years of a degree course, and also as a basis for further study. The NELP DipHE development group proposed that arrangements should be made for diplomates to enter certain existing courses in the polytechnic at the beginning of the third year of an established course. These proposals gave rise to a great deal of discussion by NELP faculty boards; doubts were raised about the ability of students who had completed a two-year course with an emphasis on general skills to cope with third-year undergraduate study in an established discipline. This was one aspect—others are noted below—of the frequently strained relationships between the school and other faculties in the polytechnic.

The NELP DipHE proposals also made provision for the development of post-diploma work within the School for Independent Study itself. Plans were made for courses leading to a first degree in Independent Study; students would be able to specialize in group work activities, or individual work, or in a combination of these. Formal proposals were submitted to the CNAA in 1976. The first undergraduate degree students, all NELP DipHE holders, were admitted in September 1976. Of the twelve who enrolled, eleven graduated in July 1977; there were five 2(i)s, five 2(ii)s and one Third. At the time of writing, the other student had not yet submitted his work for assessment.

EVALUATORY STUDY
Student and Staff Perceptions, July 1975

Background The first evaluatory study arose out of a need by the teaching staff to discover more about students' opinions of the course from the point of view of an external observer. Preliminary discussions were held with tutors during May and June 1975. The objectives of the study were to examine staff and student perceptions of the course, and especially to discover students' main criticisms of the programme; in addition, it was intended to examine staff and student requirements for feedback and monitoring.[6]

At the time of the inquiry there were 65 students in the first year of the course. These were divided into six groups for purposes of central studies activities, and to each of these groups was attached one central studies tutor. Each tutor, as well as the head of the school,[7] was interviewed individually.[8] Group discussions were held with students from each of the central studies groups.[9] Additional information on the working of the course came from several sources. Course documents were examined before the interviews with tutors began. Informal talks were held with students, and in three cases students who were keen to comment on their experiences were interviewed individually. Observation of both formal and informal interaction between staff and students took place in June and July 1975. It was possible for the evaluator to participate in the discussion of group projects in two of the central studies groups during this time. All these activities were much facilitated by the very willing co-operation of both students and tutors.[10]

Tutors' comments There was little disagreement among staff on the general aims of the NELP DipHE programme and on the differences between it and other higher education courses. A student-centred approach to learning and the availability of genuine student choice to pursue self-defined interests were the agreed central characteristics of the course. It was seen to be an explicit attempt to meet the ends achieved (if at all) as a by-product of less innovatory courses; these were said to be skills like effective working in groups, and abilities like greater self-consciousness of one's own needs and the effective and independent pursuit of one's own aims. All the tutors stressed the idea of transferability and flexibility of skills and the relevance of flexible skills to a rapidly changing society; all were in agreement, so far as the DipHE was concerned, with a reduction in the importance attached to professional and subject-based knowledge and a corresponding increase in the importance of the concepts of problem definition and solving.

In the interpretations of these general aims, however, there were substantial differences between tutors. Most of the staff were concerned by an apparent lack of agreement amongst themselves. One mentioned the fact that a hitherto existing tacit consensus on aims was now breaking down. It was possible to explore this area more fully in the interviews. Several tutors were worried that the original ideals of the programme were being compromised, but they approached the problem of devaluing of ideals from two different directions. One group interpreted the general aims of the programme in terms which echo the ideas of Carl Rogers and Abraham Maslow. The student-centred approach was seen to be concerned with the total development of the person; competence was defined as coming to terms with oneself and rejecting habitual patterns of behaviour. One of these tutors commented:

> 'We need to examine student motivation; people can do things if they believe in themselves. Their attitudes are what come first, then their skills. But the way in which we develop our students has got to be an integrated one. We must actually help people to come to terms with themselves and what makes them tick . . . you can't separate out knowledge, skills and attitudes in real life problems . . . Education is too orientated to intellectual criticism. Developing critical skills is destructive, often, to creative skills. A project can be non-intellectual, but educational.' Here he cited one of his students' group projects: 'In this case I judged students on their analytical development and their creativity.'

Another tutor from this group characterized the traditional higher education course as a 'self-justifying game' in which a minority of students was benefited at the expense of the majority; achievement was restricted because of competition which was seen by this teacher to be inimical also to growth and feeling. The unstructured nature of the NELP DipHE would, he hoped, emphasize the multi-dimensional nature of human talent and make it more difficult for people to compare themselves with each other in terms of relative worth.

The second group of tutors was troubled about the possibility of anti-intellectualism and an over-reaction to traditional methods. Personal development was not thought to be a valid end *in itself* for the DipHE:

> 'The approach which says that the DipHE is an opportunity for personal

growth and development is dangerous. One can grow and develop in a pub or a prison. Students should be encouraged to develop abilities to deal with things outside themselves. I don't want the whole thing to move into being an encounter group.'

These tutors were worried about the external credibility of the course and the students' self-indulgence in unsophisticated, haphazard 'growing', which was thought to be an irresponsible and confusing objective. These contradictory emphases on creativity as opposed to critical ability and personal as opposed to academic development undoubtedly influenced the two groups of teachers in their perceptions of student problems. It was almost as if two different models of the 'ideal student' were operating (Becker 1952). The first group believed that difficulties stemmed from a tendency to impose too many controls on students; to do their best work, students must have no constraint on the way they choose or pursue their interests. The second group thought that problems arose from too much freedom and too little context; here the view was that students would work best when confined within a fairly definite pattern of study.

The interviews revealed many differences between tutors in their attitudes to student assessment. Some attached importance to external criteria for assessment, others to student self-assessment. One tutor said that any form of qualifying assessment was bound to be uni-dimensional and that the principal effects of higher education were impossible to assess. A less extreme view, held by another tutor, was that self-assessment and peer assessment were the most crucial things, although assessment for purposes of future courses and jobs was a necessary evil which could be separated from 'real' self-assessment. Another tutor stressed the importance of external standards and publicly testable criteria for failure:

'If a course is good, nobody should fail it—but not because that's my philosophy, but because everyone should reach the standard. One can't have no assessment and then grant diplomas. It's no use saying "good" to everything . . . In the real world, when people don't do well they get thrown out or they don't succeed . . . It's doing a disservice to students to say that one should offer a diploma to someone who has vaguely "grown" as a person.'

Similar differences emerged when staff were asked to discuss the role of a tutor in the DipHE. There was agreement that the tutor's job was distinct from that of most lecturers in higher education. Responsiveness to students, creating confidence, counselling, guidance and understanding were important tasks of his which could not be avoided. Together with a substantial measure of responsibility to a group of students for the whole of their work and few clear-cut teaching methods, they were thought to make for a very demanding job. But some staff spoke of the need to provide a structure for students; others feared being too authoritarian. Some laid emphasis on the tutor as critic of his students' work: others rejected this role.

There were, of course, many differences and subtleties of emphasis in tutors' comments which have not been mentioned here. The central conflict—between structure and freedom—is to some extent a consequence of an uneasy compromise in the planning of the course between, on the one hand, the humanistic ideals of freedom to learn and the importance of emotional development in higher education, and, on the other hand, a stress on the Popperian notions of problem definition, solving, and rigorous testing. And we should remember that unease existed not only in the differences between tutors, but also in their recognition of the conflicting demands of authority and freedom made upon them as teachers in the School for Independent Study.

Students' comments Students, too, perceived the programme differently from each other; not all of them wanted the same thing from it, and their views of its problems were not uniform. The study was not designed to compare these differences in detail, although some obvious ones will be touched on below. It was certainly not possible to use the discussions as a way of comparing tutor groups. What follows concentrates on the most frequent comments of students in all of the groups.

A view expressed in all discussions was that students were experiencing a sense of isolation and unsureness because their work did not relate to other students' work. This was thought to be true especially of special interest studies but also to a considerable extent of central studies projects. Several students compared the DipHE to a more conventional course in this respect; the structure of the curriculum in the latter sort of course was felt to provide ground for discussion and communication among students, leading to a sense of 'togetherness':

> 'There's no one to talk to about what you've done on this course . . . (on other sorts of courses) if you've all got to write an essay or something, you can talk about it; if you've all been to a lecture, you can talk about it and exchange ideas.'

> 'One thing is, there's no cohesion because there's no common aim whatsoever. It's very difficult to get people together to talk about anything because they think it's not relevant to what they're doing or I think "It's not relevant to what I'm doing" . . . Therefore it's a very lonely type of course—this can be very depressing. You get no feedback on anything; you can't judge your work against anyone else's.'

The availability and interest of tutors, although valuable, was not thought to provide an adequate substitute for talking to fellow students. The comments quoted above were typical of most respondents; at the same time, it became plain during the discussions that there were at least two different orientations to the course. The extent to which it was seen as a dissatisfying experience was related to the expectations held by the two groups. At one extreme there were students who were apparently happy to accept the feeling of isolation as part of the price necessarily paid to study independently. At the other, there were students who were very anxious indeed about the lack of coherence, even to the extent of desiring the structure of a conventional course. Members of the first group tended to have had previous higher education experience; they completely rejected the usual course structures and were content to put up with parts of the course which were not directly suited to their needs in order to enjoy the benefits of the rest of the programme. Some of them, for example, thought group work was irrelevant, and wanted to concentrate full time on their special interest. A typical student of the second group was one who had no experience of higher education; he was uncommitted to and unsatisfied by the course, and was considering leaving the programme either to follow a more structured course or to abandon higher education altogether.

It would be fair to say, however, that most students who were interviewed did not fall into these two extreme categories. The majority tended towards an ambivalent attitude to the programme. The remark was often made that students' critical comments and feelings of dissatisfaction should not be taken to indicate that they wanted to exchange the freedom of choice given by the DipHE for the controls of a more conventional course; but some sort of compromise was desired. A number of those interviewed wanted a more stimulating environment for learning in which tutors acted as more than resources. One of them said:

'I don't think that they have really put enough thought into creating learning situations. I think they thought "It's a good idea, student-centred education: we'll apply it to higher education". But it's not a very stimulating environment. Staff seem to expect students to generate everything . . . they seem to have thought that students would do things like coming to them and asking for series of lectures. As I see it, an improved version of the course would be if students fitted into projects generated by staff. They ought to take more initiatives themselves . . . On an ordinary course 80 per cent of the lectures may be pretty useless, but at least they can be a source of stimulation.'

The problem of lack of cohesion and common aims was at its most acute in the views expressed by students about the level or standard of work required in the DipHE. Many respondents said that it was hard to know the standards needed, whether one's own work was at the same level as that of other students, and whether what external agencies (such as the validating and assessment boards) thought was satisfactory would be in any way related to what their tutors accepted. These problems added to the students' feelings of unsureness and confusion. Several said that the apparently different standards set in different tutor groups increased the uncertainty. Some students related this problem to a lack of feedback from their central studies and special interest tutors on their work. The DipHE documentation stressed the importance of developing problem-solving skills, and of the choice of criteria for failure and success in a project; it also emphasized the crucial role of self-assessment. We have noted above that tutors differed from each other in the amount of emphasis which they placed on these aims. It appeared from talking to students they often felt unable to test out their ideas on other people to decide their adequacy, and that the environment which would make self-assessment easy was not present.

A connected problem brought out in the discussions was that of communication. Several students were critical of the amount of time given by special interest tutors. There was a feeling expressed that the other faculties in the polytechnic were unable or unwilling to understand the DipHE, and that central studies tutors needed to maintain closer relationships with special interest tutors. The quality of communication between the head of the school and the groups was also criticized; some students thought that he did not fully understand what was actually going on in the groups.

Students were asked about the role of their tutors. There was general agreement that the tutor should be guide and referee, and someone with useful contacts in other parts of the polytechnic. But students were very conscious of differences between central studies tutors and groups, and this added to feelings of confusion about the aims of the course, to the sense of lack of cohesion, and to the perceived difficulties over expected standards of work. Worries were expressed about the fact that students in different groups were getting different ideas about the way they should be working and thinking. One difference apparent to students was the varying stress laid by tutors on academic and personal development:

> 'The group next door are completely different. We're trying to go towards an academic standard, to produce a final product. Their main interest is just trying to work in a cohesive group. That's a basic rift in the course.'

Some students were concerned that they might turn out to be 'images of their tutor', although they felt that this was happening in other groups rather than in their own. On the whole, students identified with their own tutor's aims:

> 'We obviously identify with our tutor. The other groups are images of their tutor and see the course as he sees it . . . some of the tutors have stronger personalities and tend to dictate to their groups; the tutors bring in their own ideas and the decisions are taken for the group.'

Nearly all the students interviewed were conscious of the newness of the course, and some were worried about the credibility of the DipHE in the 'outside world', relating this to the problem of levels or standards mentioned above; it was felt that success in the DipHE might not be defined as success in the outside world. Some students were less worried about the judgment of the world: 'If *I* feel I've done all right, it doesn't really bother me', one said. Certain other differences between students were apparent. Some were glad that the perceived ideals of the programme —especially in group work—had been altered by circumstance to become more 'practical'; it was said, for example, that expecting people to work together on a group project when some were less interested in it than others was not realistic. But other students were concerned that the ideals of the programme had been compromised by expediencies.

Sources of student difficulties and some suggestions The NELP DipHE provides a contrast to higher education courses in which student dissatisfaction has been traced to differences between staff and student in defining the experience of learning and teaching. Startup (1972) and Entwistle and Percy (1974), for example, noted sources of dissatisfaction arising respectively from staff emphasis on theoretical ideas and from students' perceptions of the rigid intellectual authority of the university. The DipHE explicitly mixes theoretical and commonsense ideas; the teaching situations are fluid and largely defined by students; students decide on their own objectives and are not bound by a pre-defined subject area. There is much informal interaction between staff and students, and academic and informal interactions were frequently not distinguished during the period when this study was in progress. In addition, there is apparently strong agreement between staff and students about the purposes of the course.

We might expect a course of this sort to produce, prima facie, a greater sense of community and commitment among the students than is the case on some more conventional courses. From the evidence of student discussions and staff interviews, there seem to be two reasons why this involvement might not arise. Underlying differences between staff and student might exist despite the explicitly defined agreement between them. Students were often critical, for example, of the jargon of the programme; they did not identify with what they saw to be official terms such as competence, skills, relevance, and strengths and weaknesses. One tutor was criticized for 'floating around seeing everything through a wall of educational philosophy' instead of trying to understand the difficulties students were experiencing in their project groups.

A second potential difficulty stems from the fact that an apparent concurrence between staff and student definitions will be spurious so long as students perceive differences within the staff group, and amongst themselves. If students feel, for example, that there is a lack of agreement amongst their teachers about what work is qualification for a satisfactory DipHE award, then a perception of agreement at a general level between staff and students will not make for positive evaluation and involvement with the course.

Discussions and observations during the summer of 1975 left a strong impression that student involvement in the course was made problematic by these intra-group conflicts of definitions—both students' perceptions of staff differences and students' experience of student differences. These problems were compounded by a sense of unsureness among staff and students as to exactly what their respective roles were. The consequence for many students was the growth of apathy, passivity, and doubt.

Following this evaluatory study, recommendations were made to the staff in July 1975 for possible changes to the programme. These included clearer definitions of the objectives of the course and more explicit acceptance of the possible conflicts in these objectives; clearer definitions of tutors' and students' roles, so that each group might know better what was expected of it; more explicit structuring of the course, with rather more responsibility given to tutors to provide frameworks in which students could study; better communications between the programme and other parts of the polytechnic, especially special interest tutors; better communications between students, probably assisted by a reduction in the exclusivity of central studies groups; and more precisely shared concerns about the problems worth studying and the criteria for assessing their importance among tutors.

The Operation of the Planning Period, October–November 1975

We have already noted the importance attached in the DipHE programme at NELP to the initial stages of the student's experience on the course, when his future programme of study is planned. Shortly after the planning period ended for students beginning their course in 1975, first-year students were asked to complete a questionnaire to provide feedback on their experience of the period and to examine their perceptions of the course as a whole.[11]

Although 60 per cent of the students replying to the questionnaire felt that their special interest tutor appreciated the purpose and structure of the programme, and the majority thought that their tutors did not try to exercise too much control over them, more than half said that there were disagreements between central studies tutors on the meaning and objectives of the programme. There was also some feeling—expressed by 37 per cent of students—that central studies tutors' interests outside the course adversely affected their commitment to it. About half the respondents confessed themselves unclear about the assessment procedures which would be used and a similar proportion were unsure about the standards of work required. A majority thought that they were isolated, as DipHE students, from the rest of the polytechnic; a third felt that it was also difficult to meet other DipHE students. As many as 31 per cent of the students were unclear about the objectives of the course.

Several students mentioned that they had learned from the planning period, and that they now recognized its usefulness, but most students were very critical of it. It was felt to be confusing, unstructured, badly organized, and generally frustrating:

'There have been times when it seems even the staff didn't know what they were doing.'

'It was almost deliberately misleading and confusing.'

'Can see no point at all in having the planning. I have not really planned what I really wanted.'

'It is a complete and utter waste of time and money.'

A source of difficulty appeared to be the perceived inflexibility of the planning period. Students thought that much time was spent on irrelevant work—they were especially critical of several exercises that were undertaken in group and personal development—while there was too much pressure and hurry during the last two weeks of the period, when they were required to draw up statements about their objectives for the course and their means for achieving them. There was a feeling that important decisions were being made too early and on the basis of too little experience. It was said that too little emphasis was placed on providing information on which students could make realistic choices, and too much stress was laid on jargon and dogma. Students suggested that more time might be allowed before making binding statements about objectives; that more personal help was needed from tutors on problems seen to be relevant by students (for example, the relationship between choice of objectives and future careers); and that more information was needed on the reasons for having the planning period and on what was expected from tutors and students by the end of it. Another important criticism was that students felt unable to assess effectively the range and type of special interest activities open to them during the planning period; more time was felt to be needed to choose special interest studies and special interest tutors.

The planning period, by definition, was intended to be an insecure and difficult time for students; a transition between a student's previous experiences and his course, in which ideas and values are re-directed and objectives for the future clarified. But students felt that although they had been promised relevance and guidance, both were missing; while the theoretical suppositions of the planning period were thought to be working out badly in practice. Somewhat similar comments on the structure of the course and the unclear aims of the programme, and on different views of the course by different central studies tutors, were made by these students and by students in the previous year of the course (see above, pp 22-23). There was a danger that the planning period might set a tone of misunderstanding and insecurity which would then inform the remainder of a student's programme.

To some extent the very critical comments made by students might be attributable to the critical and independent attitude of individuals choosing to follow a NELP DipHE programme. A sizeable number of students felt that the period, and the course as a whole, could be substantially improved. In particular, it was thought that the planning period could be better arranged to meet individual needs; that more personal guidance should be offered during it; that more honesty was required in describing the realities of the programme, before students began it; and that clearer statements of the aims of the course and of what was expected from students should be given. Better liaison was wanted with other faculties during the planning period, more information on assessment procedures, and fuller details of how to work effectively in project groups. Disagreements between tutors about the purposes of the programme, and students' perceptions of the effects of these disagreements, were further difficulties.

Other Comments on the Course

It would be unfair to confine the discussion of the NELP DipHE programme to the findings of the evaluation studies which concentrated on staff and student perceptions. Reference needs to be made to the remarks of other observers of the programme, and in particular to the comments of external examiners on the standard of students' work and on the structure of the programme after its first two years of operation.

Student performance There are three important questions to be examined in a consideration of student performance in the NELP DipHE. To what extent had students met their own objectives? How far had students moved towards self-direction and independence in learning? And to what extent was the standard of performance of a diploma equivalent to that of an undergraduate at the end of the second year of a degree course?

The endemic problems of comparability of objectives and the external credibility of different and self-defined aims for a course such as the NELP DipHE, which have been touched upon above, make these questions difficult ones to answer. The external examiners were very aware of these problems and several commented on their own lack of experience in moderating results from innovatory programmes of this sort. Equivalence of standard with second-year undergraduate level work was thought to be difficult because of the varying purposes defined in different universities for the second year, and because of the fact that certain areas of study undertaken by DipHE students were not those covered in university courses. In one case, an examiner compared students' performance with his expectations of students beginning the third-year independent studies course at Lancaster and approved the standard of diplomates' work in these terms. Several examiners commented on the exceptionally high standards achieved by the best diplomates, especially in their individual work (that is, the products of their special interest studies). One examiner remarked that the standard attained by all diplomates could be unhesitatingly equated with second-year degree level in terms of general conceptual maturity as well as ability to tackle topics in depth and to work independently. Variety, imagination, and excitement were seen to be key attributes of the best work. On the other hand, one examiner was disappointed by the poor quality of contributions from the weaker candidates, which he felt to be more than averagely unsatisfactory in comparison with undergraduate students' work.

An assessment of students' success in achieving their own objectives is not easy because of the variety of level; some were considered by the examiners to be almost trivial, and not suitable for second-year university work, no matter how they were pursued; others were thought to be excessively ambitious. It was not, however, thought to be the case that students who set themselves low objectives stood the greatest chance of being awarded a diploma. But in some cases examiners remarked that in debatable situations the distinction between levels of aims might favour students with modest aims. A problem identified by several examiners was the lack of a relationship between the validation of students' objectives and their later examination. A closer involvement with validation might help examiners to appreciate better the way in which the student set his objectives and lead to more effective moderation. Another difficulty noted by one examiner was the extent to which it was reasonable to expect some objectives to be achieved: by definition, he remarked, we seldom, if ever, achieve our own best objectives.

It was felt that the difficulty of measuring the extent to which students had achieved independence was a particularly severe problem. It was no doubt aggravated by the programme's lack of an explicit definition of independence. One examiner noted that the students to whom he talked were unusually ready to defend their attitudes and ideas, although he felt that in their group assessments students were not able to appreciate the methodological problems of the social science perspectives which they adopted: they were not aware of what they did not know. This criticism is reflected in the remarks made by another examiner to the effect that students had difficulty in coping with basic problems in independent study such as the interpretation of data, effective use of libraries, and effective communication. It was suggested that the department needed to specify standards in these fields as a precondition for helping students to perceive what they need to learn, and thereby to enable them to increase their choice and independence. A further relevant consideration in measuring independence was each student's starting-point in his course. For while some needed careful structuring of their learning at the beginning so that they gradually became more and more independent, others were already independent learners: how were their different outcomes at the end of the course to be assessed?

Assessment Some of the problems in the assessment schemes in use in 1976 are implicit in the comments made above. In addition, several examiners commented on the format of the group work assessment, in which students work together on a defined group task and are then assessed in terms of their individual contributions. Some students were much dissatisfied with the artificial nature of the set situation; it was suggested by one examiner that the purpose of the exercise—to test their methodological rigour and ability to contribute individual skills to the group output, rather than to assess a product—had not been made sufficiently clear to them. Another felt that future group assessments ought to be more flexible and made less stressful for those students who were inhibited or frustrated by group work.

We have already considered above the difficulties experienced by students on the programme in coming to terms with the assessment schemes and in appreciating the standards of work required from them. In the schemes used in the first two years of the programme, a particular difficulty seemed to be the absence of an obvious relationship between the process of peer and self-assessment and that of final qualifying assessment. One examiner referred to some cases in which students were presenting work for final assessment which was clearly not of an adequate standard and which should have been identified as such earlier in the course. The freedom the students enjoyed needed to be constrained by indications of what work was going to be acceptable.

The course and its environment The difficulty of effectively relating the DipHE programme to other courses and departments, and to other staff and students within the polytechnic, has been noted by several observers. The problem has been identified above in terms of students' perceptions of isolation from other faculties and other students in the college. It has also manifested itself in the physical distance of the school from other parts of the polytechnic, in strained relationships between some special interest tutors and their students, and in other faculties' doubts about the ability of DipHE diplomates to achieve Honours degree standards in post-diploma work in particular disciplines.

During the first year of the NELP DipHE, even a casual observer of the school would not have failed to recognize a considerable ésprit de corps among its members. Students and staff alike were conscious of an involvement in a radical experiment in higher education, and were quick to defend its value. No doubt the solidarity arising from a common cause did much to mitigate the effects of the disagreements on aims that we discussed in the earlier part of this chapter. The political distance between the school and the polytechnic, a phenomenon to some extent consciously created by the organizers of the course in their emphasis on the innovatory nature of the programme, was expressed in a number of ways. Students felt that they were different from other polytechnic students, and that they were seen as outsiders; staff views of the course and the interest shown by external visitors and observers of the school during the first two years reinforced this self-image. Students expressed fears, reported by external examiners and others (Allen and Draper 1975; Eaton 1976) about the failure of certain special interest tutors to give useful guidance and co-operation. It was thought that special interest tutors frequently had little sympathy with DipHE students' particular difficulties and that they did not understand the concept of integration between the general skills of central studies and specialist work. Indeed, the basis for integration between special interest and central studies was never explicitly laid down during the first two years. For many students they remained distinct activities.

There is little doubt that many staff outside the school perceived the presence of the DipHE programme within the polytechnic as a threat to established academic procedures. A special source of acrimony was the formulation of post-diploma programmes and the support of existing courses for future BA independent study students. Thus one Faculty Development Committee reported on the BA proposal: [12]

'While recognizing the value of independent study, the Development Committee was doubtful that this could readily achieve degree-level standard without appropriate grounding in relevant disciplines. While the proposal makes reference to using disciplines in the formulation and solution of problems, the Committee was not satisfied that the programme or the previous DipHE course made adequate provision for students to obtain mastery of the theory and methodology of these disciplines or provision for assessing that this had been achieved.'

(NELP No date)

The same committee had an icy comment to make on the standards expected from independent study students:

'The Committee thought it was difficult to establish objective criteria of assessment for individual programmes of study. Without such commonly recognized and externally comparable standards, it was thought that there was a danger of standards of attainment becoming, in effect, negotiable, so that what would be deemed acceptable would be what students had in fact succeeded in doing. Pressure on students to achieve a given level of competence, and also to achieve a given volume of work, might therefore be less than in other courses . . . It was thought there was no evidence offered that students, having completed this course, would in fact have a level of competence equal to third year Honours students.'

It is instructive to compare these comments, with their emphasis on external motivation, established disciplinary boundaries, and objective academic standards, with the positions expressed by DipHE tutors in a previous section of this chapter. We can imagine their reaction without difficulty. But the existence of tensions of this sort, whether explicitly stated or tacit, led to much anxiety among students about their position in the polytechnic and about the reality of post-diploma opportunities.

CONCLUSION
It is important that we conclude this chapter by emphasizing that the evaluation studies described above were expressly designed to reveal difficulties which students and staff might be undergoing during the experimental phase of the NELP DipHE. They might, for this reason, be thought to present a somewhat partial picture. Undoubtedly they abstract from the complex reality of the course its principal problems at that time. Students were highly critical of the organization of the programme, but there is little doubt that the majority of them learned a great deal from their experience in the school. Quite apart from the high academic standards achieved by many students, other benefits were directly related to the conflicts and difficulties we have mentioned. This is especially true so far as gains in personal awareness and improvements in relationships with others are concerned. Interviews of students who began their DipHE programmes in 1976, carried out shortly before they completed the course,[13] show that they valued the freedom provided them; they spoke of gaining increased confidence and self-discipline through their experiences, of becoming less afraid of dealing with people in positions of authority, and of developing the ability to confront issues rather than avoid them.

Since the studies described in this chapter were completed, many changes have been made to the way in which the DipHE is organized. Several of them took place as a result of the comments made by students; the principal amendments are summarized in Chapter 4.

NOTES
[1] This is not the place to discuss the strengths and weaknesses of the binary policy and the NELP ideology as strategies for the planning of post-compulsory education. Some of the more vocal advocates of the NELP ideology have sometimes shown a tendency to see the business of higher education in violently polarized terms, so that 'academic' knowledge cannot be 'useful' and institutes of higher education cannot both reflect the needs of the community and communicate academic knowledge. A transparently combative tactic—the

propensity to define one's own approach to teaching and course organization as new and unique—has also sometimes characterized the NELP attempts to define a distinctive approach. For discussions of the problems of binarism, see Lukes (1967) and Trow (1972).

[2] It is interesting to compare the only other DipHE programme beginning in 1974 with the NELP scheme. At Bulmershe College of Higher Education (then known as Berkshire College of Higher Education) a different approach to fulfilling the main recommendations of the government's guidelines was taken. A unit-based course structure was adopted which fitted closely with the college's BEd degree scheme, so that students effectively completed the first two years of the degree course. A much higher proportion of the entrants than at NELP had two 'A' levels.

[3] The pitfalls in this argument are exposed by Lewis (1978).

[4] Students aged 21 or under, without 'A' levels.

[5] The success of this kind of procedure can partly be judged by some of the comments made by students in the evaluation studies which are reported later in this chapter.

[6] These latter comments are not included in this report.

[7] In what follows 'tutors' should be taken to include the head of the school.

[8] These interviews took place between 2 and 13 June 1975. They were not formally structured, but it was ensured that several questions were raised at each one concerning staff interpretations of the official definitions of the course appearing in the CNAA submission and similar documents, about the difference between the programme and other courses in higher education, about a tutor's role as a teacher on the DipHE, and about student assessment. The interviews varied in length from thirty minutes to one hour. They were tape-recorded and summaries were later written by the interviewer.

[9] There were held between 13 June and 7 July 1975. The choice of students was non-random; arrangements were made with each group for a discussion to be held, usually by attending a central studies group meeting a few days before, and as many students as were interested were invited to attend. In most cases, four or five members of each group were present. The most likely source of bias in the responses is that only the most committed students talked to the interviewer, in that they were the ones most often present at college. Students mentioned on several occasions the fact that certain group members were rarely present at meetings of project groups. The discussions which took place lasted from twenty minutes to forty-five minutes and were tape-recorded; summary transcripts were later prepared. Students were asked to concentrate on what they thought were the good and bad features of the course, to consider their own and their tutors' roles on the course, and to comment on assessment procedures.

[10] We emphasize that the comments made by staff and students refer to the first four terms of the course's operation, when the programme was in its first, experimental phase; they should not be interpreted as illustrating its present structure.

[11] The principal issues investigated by this questionnaire were ones raised by the previous intake of students during the interview studies reported above. In closed-ended questions, students were asked to comment on their perceptions of assessment procedures, on their relationships with their tutors, on the DipHE and the polytechnic environment, on course structure and objectives, and on their relationships with other students. Respondents were also asked to answer open-ended questions about their experience of the planning period and to offer suggestions for changes which they would like to see made. A total of fifty-nine questionnaires was completed (response rate 61 per cent).

[12] There has been an interesting shift of emphasis in the faculties' reactions to the BA degree

32

by independent study since 1976. In 1976, some faculties felt that they would not be able to exercise control over the programmes of study authorized to take place within them by a registration board (see page 54) dominated by the SIS. The faculties now have more power within the board and increasingly resent the control over them exercised by its external members.

[13] By the school's own researchers to explore the benefits experienced by students during their stay there.

STUDENT PROGRESS: DipHE 1974 ENTRANTS

Table 1   WITHDRAWAL RATE

	'A' level or equivalent	Mature	'Non-standard'*	Totals
Withdrew before final assessment	6	11	4	21
Entered for assessment 1975	23	23	6	52
TOTALS	29	34	10	73

*See note 4, page 31

Table 2   OUTCOME OF FINAL ASSESSMENTS

	'A' level or equivalent	Mature	'Non-standard'*	Totals
Pass	19	19	5	43
Conditional Pass	3	3	0	6
Fail	1	1	1	3
TOTALS	23	23	6	52

*See note 4, page 31

THE ORIGINS OF THE SCHEME

In March 1973 the senate of the University of Lancaster approved the proposal that a School of Independent Studies should be established. This followed three years of discussion and planning by a small group of academic staff (consisting mainly of younger lecturers) and negotiation with the senate and its representatives. The scheme of independent studies as finally accepted was far different from that originally envisaged by the planning group.

During 1970 a fluid and informal group of lecturers in the university met to discuss various topics of educational interest. The stimulus for the meetings had been an induction/training course for university teachers which had recently been organized at Lancaster; some participants felt that issues about university teaching had been raised which should be pursued further. The convenor of the meetings during the early months was a lecturer in the Department of Educational Research, Wacek Koc. He had been the director of the training course and, interestingly, had been one of the first academic appointments in the university in 1964—appointed specifically to research developments in university teaching methods. Koc helped to give structure to early meetings by preparing discussion papers. During 1970 and 1971 the size of the discussion group varied between fifteen and thirty members, almost all of whom were from the humanities and social sciences. The vice-chancellor of the university was invited to attend a number of meetings and did so, contributing significantly to early discussions.

Lancaster, like all the new universities of the early 1960s, was founded amidst an outpouring of rhetoric about the need to develop new kinds of undergraduate courses and more effective undergraduate teaching methods. This group of staff, in their initial discussions, evidently felt that Lancaster innovations had only partially succeeded: they were concerned about the success of their own teaching, about the apparent lack of motivation among some students, and about the appropriateness of the same teaching methods to students at the end, as well as at the beginning, of an undergraduate career. The group also felt strongly about the 'false isomorphism'[2] which existed between subjects, departments and disciplines. To a great extent, they argued in early papers, undergraduate courses were standardized intellectual units. The possibilities for students of variation and experimentation were limited by the requirements of equivalence and uniformity in the assessment of work for Honours degrees.

Nevertheless, Lancaster courses were structured in a much more flexible manner than was the case with the older civic universities. After a three-subject first year, students did have the opportunity to change their originally intended major field of study. What was needed, concluded the group, were further innovations, particularly in teaching, to build on the existing structural flexibility of the university and provide for some students the opportunity of a study programme that was as open-ended as their developing motivation dictated. Thus, in early 1971, the discussions of the group began to centre upon the idea of a school of independent studies.

The name 'independent studies' emerged from the group's exploration of American attempts to relate courses to student's interests and motivations. A wide range of ideas on the form a school of independent studies might have were debated. Most members were agreed that the school should aim at providing additional opportunities for learning which crossed the existing divisions between courses and subjects, and that this should be combined with chances of studying a particular topic in greater depth than was normally possible. Thus a situation would have to be created in which study schemes could be individually determined. Since the approach would be student- and problem-centred, rather than course-centred, a greater degree of interdisciplinary contact and interaction would be achieved.

The structure which a school of independent studies might appropriately take was a source of much heated discussion within the group and was to prove the greatest stumbling block in the scheme before it found acceptance with the senate of the university. Most members of the group believed that the intellectual atmosphere which they would want to see developed could only survive in a new kind of structure in which students were treated as mature, motivated learners and, as one discussion paper put it:

'. . . the notion of "staff" setting work, "students" doing it, and "staff" assessing it and handing it back, and the "student" putting it away, would be one academic tradition that could hopefully be lost.'

There should be no head of the school, it was proposed, rather a democratic assembly of all students and staff to take ultimate responsibility for every decision. As ideas became more concrete, it emerged that the group were thinking of 'the creation within the University of an autonomous section', with a body of about one hundred students taking the final two years of their degree course there. The original plan suggested that six full-time staff plus the equivalent of six half-time teachers from various departments and 'a number of dedicated souls about the university who might help out with the odd student' would be necessary.

By the spring term of 1972 the group had prepared a general discussion document for the information of interested parties in the university and a set of proposals to be put to senate. The discussion document carefully differentiated the Lancaster proposals from 'the majority of American independent study programmes' which, it said, were concerned with 'organizing the independent study of prescribed curricula'. The origins of the Lancaster proposals were related to the growth of knowledge which, it was asserted, made numerous curricula possible for students in any area, to campus unrest in the late 1960s, and to 'the end of paternalism in relation to student learning arrangements, mores and deferential attitudes to institutional authority (which) prompted the re-examination of the educational process itself and the desire for it to have more immediate meaning and more intellectual promise'. The Lancaster scheme was 'based rather on the motivational aspects of most learning theories which converge almost to the point of consensus in relating interest to learning effectiveness'. 'The proposed alternative', at Lancaster, 'allows the student, with the best possible advice, to work out what he feels he needs to know'. The document's description of the student learning in the proposed school and of the role of staff is crucially significant:

> 'The idea of the independent route is to help the student to become self-sufficient as a learner: teaching is needed less and less as he gains experience and confidence. But no uniform change could be expected in all cases. Instead of being uniform, the nature and intensity of the teaching contact alters in accordance with the changing individual need. Although some students would experience more of it than they would during course work, the total need within the School should grow progressively less as the attitudes of self-help develop.'

It is interesting that the writers of the document listed 'several very specific fears' which:

> '. . . were expressed in the planning discussions and in canvassed comments: that the School would cream off the best students, that it would create an élite, become a haven for middle class dilettanti or academic weaklings, or a refuge for anarchists, drop-outs and playboys. Some people expressed concern about there being any further (University) initiative on development in view of the limited resources, others disliked any more proliferation of study options and expected over-divergence or over-concentration by students, also lack of discipline, lack of structure and lack of results.'

As it happened, spring term of 1972 was not an auspicious time for any radical proposals to be put to the Lancaster senate. That term saw major student troubles at Lancaster, including two occupations of the administration building (which caused expensive damage) and a boycott of classes. Senate was criticized from all sides for its role in the affair. Its likely attitude towards the far-reaching independent studies proposals could not be predicted. Sympathetic senior members of the university advised the independent studies group to wait.

Nevertheless, in April 1972 the proposals for this new kind of academic community were put to senate and the proposers emphasized that they were seeking to achieve the same goals of flexibility, balance and depth in academic study as the founding fathers of the university. In fact, senate discussed the proposals temperately and asked for clarification of a number of issues: eg, the ability of undergraduate students to plan their courses, the timing of a transfer to independent study, and the cost of the scheme and its comparability to other courses of study. Encouraged, the planning group sent a further document to senate in June 1972, answering the questions and making the politically apt suggestion that the school be introduced for a trial period of at least five years. The senate referred the proposals to other parts of the university for comment.

The planning group canvassed views on their ideas from outside the university by sending one of their documents to a long list of distinguished academics in this country, in the United States, and elsewhere. The replies that came back were broadly favourable to the scheme and wished the planning group success. Among the comments made by these distinguished outsiders can be found regrets that the scheme would probably be emasculated by assessment for an Honours degree, that the relationship of student and tutor would be crucial because there would be no 'department' to watch over the student, that a vital concern would be for adequate controls over academic standards and that there was value in having an 'experimental unit' in every university.

Senates are not the best places to stage debates on complex educational issues and it appears that at no time in 1972–1973 did the Lancaster senate discuss in detail the philosophy and fundamental assumptions of the scheme. Comments were largely on organizational, structural and procedural points, on questions of economics and on implications for the rest of the university. Clearly the majority of science and applied science professors regarded the scheme as a further product of inexact, non-scientific thinking. One made the written comment:

'I find it impossible to deduce from the memorandum what 'independent studies' means.'

He asked the proposers:

'. . . to explain clearly what it is all about.'

Other written comments from members of senate at this time included worries (some of them very familiar to the planning group) that the proposed school would 'skim the cream off the milk' (ie take the best-motivated students), that it was unfair to leave to students—as had been proposed—the choice of whether to have classified or unclassified degrees, that the staff-student ratio required by the school would be at the expense of the rest of the university, and that it was unacceptable to have students selecting their own form of assessment.

As the comments came in, the planning group in mid-1972 began to divide. Some felt that they would be forced to compromise their ideas too far, others that they were tired of drafting new documents. Nevertheless, the remainder put a revised paper to senate in October 1972. The document laid great stress on the group's desire 'to ensure the maintenance of academic standards and efficient administration' and emphasized that such innovations in the university's structure as were proposed were 'an integral part of the educational aims of the school'. The earliest document put to senate had incautiously stated that the group felt the school would serve as a 'catalyst' for change in the university. This assertion was now dropped and the major compromises at this stage were to accept that the school should have a head (a director appointed from the staff) and that degrees should be classified. Nevertheless one member of the senate attacked the compromise scheme fiercely as an attempt 'to drive a wedge into the existing university structure', to allow students 'to have the kudos of an honours degree but without the discipline of an examination', and to encourage doubtful academic work which would be no more 'than random excursions into any subjects which attracted the student's fancy'.

Senate now (October 1972) voted to approve the 'educational value of a programme of independent studies' but again referred the proposals back to the planning group with specific questions about resources, organization, career prospects for full-time staff in independent studies, comparability of assessment, and prospects of graduate study for independent studies majors.

The planning group was now in considerable disarray, sensing that specific proposals would not be approved by senate without a considerable reduction of the staff resources proposed as essential and without the possible appointment of a director of the school from outside the group itself or the staff who might volunteer to work in it. Nevertheless, in February 1973 the questions posed by senate were answered in great detail. The group decided to bring the structure of the school into line with conventional university practice but still urged that on resources they were 'intentionally asking that the school be treated slightly more generously'. A scheme based on 'units of assessment' lasting for the final four terms of the undergraduate career was now proposed. The senate sent the scheme to the Development Committee to review practical and resource implications in the light of advice from the vice-chancellor and the academic registrar. At the Development Committee representatives of the planning group found themselves arguing unsuccessfully against the creation of a committee of independent studies containing senate representatives to oversee the school, against the external advertising of the post of director of the school, and against a conventional allocation of staffing resources. However, the final compromises were made and, after a vote, the senate in March 1973 established the school with the status of a university department and with the requirements that the ratio of staff should not be different from that of the rest of the university, that the post of director should be advertised externally, and that the scheme should be reviewed during the academic year 1976–77.

The persistence of the planning group had finally been rewarded. Many of its members were disappointed with the limitations placed upon the school, but at least now there was a new dimension to the undergraduate teaching of the university. In July 1973 a director of the school was appointed from a long list of applicants. He was Frank Oldfield, a geographer who was, at the time of appointment, deputy vice-chancellor of an overseas university. He had been a lecturer at Lancaster in its early years and in his late twenties had moved from there to a chair in Northern Ireland, where he became dean of faculty. That Oldfield was already known and respected by many senior members of the university, and that he had held chairs in other universities, were important facts in promoting the acceptability of the school throughout the university in its first two years. Oldfield could not take up his new post for several months and the position of acting director was filled by Jane Routh, a lecturer in the Sociology department who transferred to the school. Oldfield remained director for a year and a half and during that time was appointed to a personal chair. On his resignation, Jane Routh—remaining at lecturer status—was appointed director.

The first six students were provisionally registered as majors in October 1973. They were chosen through an ad hoc procedure, devised and supervised by senate.

THE OPERATION OF THE INDEPENDENT STUDIES SCHEME AT LANCASTER

Course Structure at Lancaster University[3]

The new campus-based universities of the 1960s were founded with a commitment to broader patterns of undergraduate study. At Lancaster all first-year undergraduates take three subjects of equal weighting and have to achieve a satisfactory standard in each (Part 1). Part 2 occupies the remaining two years of undergraduate study and is concentrated on the students' single major course (one main subject) or combined major course (two or three main subjects). The classified Honours degree is awarded at the end of Part 2 and based on nine 'units of study', ie assessed courses. One of these nine units—the so-called Free Ninth Unit—is available for students to take in a subject remote from their main field of interest. There are some variations in this pattern, mainly for science students, but the broad framework is the same for all. Lancaster has a departmental structure and the single major degree schemes, which the majority of students follow, are based within the departments. Cognate departments are organized into boards of studies, which approve new courses and course changes and facilitate inter-departmental degree schemes.

It was into this academic structure that the School of Independent Studies was now fitted. It was placed alongside the boards of studies under its own senate subcommittee. The procedures established in 1973/4 for the recruitment of students were kept as simple as possible. Students were encouraged to express an interest in independent study towards the end of their Part 1 course. A student met a member of the full-time staff of the school,[4] outlined his ideas for an Independent Studies project and explained his reasons for wishing to undertake it. If the staff member felt that the proposed scheme had possibilities the student was encouraged to prepare a written outline of it. An appropriate director of studies—probably a staff member in another department—was approached and the scheme put to him. If he agreed to act as director of studies, the proposed scheme went to the Committee for Independent Studies[5] at its first meeting in the student's second year. The committee then made recommendations to the school.

If 'provisionally accepted', the students registered for a normal major/minor Part 2 scheme, and started independent studies as their Free Ninth Unit. They thus spent part of the next two terms (the equivalent of one course—the Free Ninth Unit) defining and working towards a period of full-time independent study to be carried out during the last four terms of Part 2. From October to January of the second year the students worked on their plans with their directors, and sought to prepare a substantial piece of evidence to show that they were capable of doing what they had planned to do. They were expected to search for resources, compile a bibliography and propose an assessment scheme. This was presented to the Committee for Independent Studies in February of the second year. Students who proposed to continue to do a 'major' (6/9 of the total degree assessment) or 'minor' (introduced in 1974 and constituting 2/9 or 3/9 of the total assessment) in independent studies prepared more detailed outlines and presented more substantial pieces of work. The committee read the whole submission and supporting reports from the students' departments—to simplify the process and to make it more reliable sub-committees were later formed—and then decided whether the topic was acceptable, whether the proposed scheme was feasible, and whether the student appeared likely to cope with independent study. The committee might accept or reject a scheme, or request modifications or further evidence.[6] Students who were not accepted for independent studies, or who withdrew, reverted to their normal Part 2 scheme.[7] The remainder carried out their chosen, and carefully planned, independent studies projects for the next four terms until the time came to present the outcome of the work for assessment and degree classification.

Process of Selection
Thus admission to the Lancaster School of Independent Studies could and can only be secured after a rigorous process of selection, both formal and informal. The selection process is based on the idea that there is both 'self-selection' on the part of the student himself (who is encouraged at all stages to evaluate his own progress and suitability for independent study) and selection by the school.

The criteria for selection are crucial. One of the full-time staff of the school admitted[8] that he was 'not confident' that they knew precisely what they were looking for, or that 'they were able to categorize the successful independent studies students', but in broad terms, students should show evidence of being 'strongly motivated, but able to organize time well, disciplined, sufficiently open minded to take advice from people who might have a different view. They must be successful and patient'. Motivation and the relationships between student and director of studies are obviously important. A full-time member of the school meets with both to form a judgment on whether they will work well together.

The school emphasizes that it does not accept only students with high marks in Part I. In theory, at least, it holds to the philosophy that students of different levels of academic ability, conventionally measured, are able to benefit from the experience of independent study. It is arguable, however, that the kinds of preparatory submissions required before acceptance necessitate a significant level of ability, as well as of motivation, on the part of the student. Many of the independent studies students accepted in the early years proved to be older, mature students who had come to university with clear ideas of their interests, pre-university experience upon which to draw, and self-confidence.

In each year there has been a large difference between the number of students who want to do independent studies and the number finally accepted. On average the school receives approximately 150 enquiries from first-year students. Of these only about 80 make further enquiries and eventually about 60 submit outlines. About 40 of these will find directors of studies. The school aims at finally accepting about 15 majors and 20 minors.

Assessment

The school expects that there will be a great divergence in the modes of work adopted by students, and in the approaches to supervision taken by directors of studies. Some students will want to work virtually alone; others will seek out courses in different parts of the university and ask permission to sit in on them. Some will want to consult not only their director of studies but other staff members when it seems that the latter might be a useful resource. Some directors will require students to attend weekly; others when the students feel the need. In an early note, however, the school warned directors that they should be 'sufficiently well aware of what a student is doing to pick up any problems before they develop seriously'.

All students and directors, however, work within the same framework of assessment and a common awareness that in May of the final year the student must present the fruits of his independent work for assessment for degree classification. Assessment is based on the normal university 'units of assessment' structure. Thus, while an independent studies major accounts for six-ninths of the student's final degree assessment, the student stipulates how this proportion is to be made up—how it is to be weighted. Final decisions about weighting have to be made by the February of the third year and approved by the school. Students may also stipulate in what form the work is to be presented: eg, as a dissertation, group of dissertations, or series of essays. The work may include one or more examination papers and some practical or experiential work.

The work as finally submitted is assessed by the director of studies and by one or more other internal examiners, all marking independently. All sets of marks go with the complete file of a student's work to the external examiner who makes the final judgment. There is one main external examiner for the School of Independent Studies but in cases where this examiner thinks the subject area is beyond his competence he calls on other external examiners, normally those being used by other departments in the university.

EVALUATORY STUDY

The remainder of this chapter is based on a small-scale evaluation of the first three years of the School of Independent Studies carried out during the spring and summer of 1976.[9]

The Success of Independent Studies

Certainly, the lecturers, students, senior members of the university and external examiners, when asked, agreed that the School of Independent Studies at Lancaster had proved to be a success. What they meant by 'success' evidently varied. For some it was simply the case that what had at first appeared to be a radical and threatening innovation had been peacefully assimilated into the structure of the university. It affected only a few students but helped to give the university the image of being in the forefront of educational development. Others, without looking too closely at the detail, observed that the school was evidently meeting a need: some students were demonstrably capable of studying 'independently' and doing good work. At Lancaster they now had the opportunity.

Questions about the standard and the scope of the independent studies work done in the school are difficult to answer satisfactorily. At a superficial level, the results have been good. In the first year of graduates there were three First Class degrees achieved out of a group of six graduates and in the second the twelve graduates achieved one First, seven Seconds and four Thirds.[10] The external examiner wrote that 'the general standard of work in independent study had tended to be somewhat higher than that of other undergraduates. This is probably to be expected because the students are self-selected (and thus very committed) and then selected by the school in terms of their ability to work satisfactorily on an independent project . . . All the work I have seen so far shows considerable creativity and experimentation.' However, he also commented that 'the numbers of students should probably be kept fairly small, since this kind of work is far from suiting all undergraduates (and one or two students might have done better in a conventional course)'. These comments relate only, of course, to the written work presented at the end of the course, rather than to any attempt to evaluate the student as a developing independent learner.

The topics, or areas of study, chosen by independent studies students have, largely, been recognizably within the arts and social science areas. The limited number of science/mathematics projects relates to some lack of sympathy in that area of the university and, no doubt, to the more closed structure of the science student's course from the time he enters the university. Many of the topics chosen by independent studies students give the appearance of not ranging beyond a number of closely related disciplines: eg 'Transport economics and injury and accident causation'; 'Military technology and systems'; 'Social dynamism and state theory—an examination of sociological views of social class'; 'Existentialism—18th-century German philosophy and religion'. Some of the topics chosen by independent studies majors are indistinguishable—in title at least—from those which might have been selected by postgraduate research students: eg 'Dualism and non-dualism as a basis of God-talk'; 'Poetic method and structure in the Cantos of Ezra Pound'; 'Vernacular architecture'. Analysis of student records demonstrates that the majority of students follow topics which are related to the intended major courses for which they registered on entry to the university. Thus the subjects students study in the first year do generally feed into their independent studies work and they do not generally embark upon projects without some background knowledge and skills. What appears to be happening in the selection of independent studies topics is that, freed from the ordinary attendance and coursework requirements of a conventional major course, students are able to concentrate upon particular areas which they define as of significance or interest to themselves. The topics may, or may not, be pursued outside the confines of particular or related disciplines.

A key issue in the early debates on independent studies has been whether the planning group were trying to construct an 'alternative society' within the university—put more bluntly, opponents of independent studies were afraid that the school would primarily attract left-wing students and topics. Now, after observing the scheme for three years, a senior professor observed that, indeed:

'. . . there has been a concentration of students who are left of the political spectrum. I would have thought that that was very natural in the sense that this is not a normal pattern of university behaviour . . . If we were to go beyond that and say that the kind of work that has been done has a strong political slant in its content, then I think this would be true in a small degree.'

But the key factor, the senior member went on, was the provision for such students of directors of studies who:

'. . . are able to understand the kind of concepts or interests which students of this kind have . . . nevertheless themselves have an effective critical relationship or attitude towards it and are able to encourage the students to develop this critical faculty.'

The more diffuse views of students and of directors of studies give some 'feel' of the success of independent studies as a process, and as an end in itself, rather than as a means to production of pieces of written work for final assessment. Students were unanimous in their agreement that independent study had been a worthwhile experience for them; all would choose to study independently again; some of them claimed that they would have left university if the opportunity for independent study had not presented itself. One student said 'as a learning experience it was tremendous. It has made me more mature', and another enthused that 'it has been an enriching and broadening two years for me'. But such comments are very general— what did students claim specifically that independent studies had done for them?

Probably the most important outcome asserted by many of the students was that independent study gave them the opportunity to do original, creative work. Many of them were scathing in their criticisms of conventional courses in which, they felt, there was little opportunity for critical thought or original expression. One student noted that 'he was creating something rather than following someone else's ideas'. These views are supported by the external examiner's judgement that 'all the work I have seen so far shows considerable creativity and experimentation'. Nevertheless, it is worth emphasizing that the dissertations and papers submitted by independent studies students at Lancaster, while in content, perhaps, demonstrating originality and creativity, show very little evidence of experimentation in the form or mode of presentation. The conventional dissertations and collections of essays predominate.

Another important outcome of the experience of independent study reported by this group of students was their sustained, or indeed increased, motivation for study, for being learners pursuing a self-defined topic of importance. One of the first students described how independent study was not just another university course which had to be passed:

> '. . . it became a part of me from the start. The structure surrounding it and the relationship with my tutor made it such that it wasn't something which I divorced from my social life.'

There were many of the other students who were equally highly motivated and one of the outstanding features of the interviews with directors of studies was each one's apparent conviction that his student must be exceptional in his degree of motivation. Such motivation was sometimes made manifest by students defining a need to go beyond the university resources, to travel to specialist libraries or museums, sometimes at their own expense, to pursue their topic properly.

The directors of studies were equally enthusiastic in their discussion of the outcomes of independent study for their students, but they made a different emphasis and talked largely of intellectual development. One observed that his students' 'rate of intellectual change' was great; another that his student had developed 'research skills' and 'a more critical approach to data and to other research that had been done'. One with experience of several independent students felt they 'had to articulate and express their ideas more than they might have chosen to do in the context of normal course structure'. One director of study was enthusiastic in his belief that his student was 'doing a more creative job of self-expression than normal'. Some directors emphasized what, essentially, were the benefits of an opportunity to specialize in a particular interest—as one put it, normal courses would not have enabled his student 'to get to grips with his subject in the same way'. Several of the Lancaster directors commented that independent study enabled students to develop the ability to solve problems. One observed that:

> '. . . my experience is that students in ordinary courses never experience anything as a genuine problem and equally never see what it is that is a solution about the solutions they present in essays.'

In independent study he felt that as the students themselves selected the problems they were more concerned to understand and solve them. This 'problem-relevance' was the most important aspect of the course.

A different, and perhaps less commonly anticipated, outcome of independent study was the positive effect which some directors observed the scheme to be having upon themselves. One of them (who was critical of various aspects of independent study) agreed that 'a lecturer could become a more rounded and effective teacher' as a result of his participation in the school. Many directors would subscribe to the view expressed by one, that:

'I have found enormous benefit in interacting with students who are coherent, motivated, reasonably mature and interested in what they are doing. It has helped me to understand the patterns of motivation and the problems of mature students and of radical students much more than before.'

Another believed his conception of university teaching had been changed:

'. . . what directors are doing is coming out from behind their fortified emplacements. If a student is involved in his work he may very well end up knowing more about the subject than you do. This challenges the authoritarian role as you are listening in a learning way to someone much younger than yourself.'

Difficulties in Independent Studies

Despite the enthusiasms of students and staff for the experience of independent studies, there were problems and difficulties which both groups perceived clearly. Some of these problems, in the judgement of students, affected their educational experience. It seems reasonable to conclude that many arose from the variety of conceptions of independent study, and of the procedures and relationships that should accompany it, which co-existed in the school. Of course there is a logical dilemma in calling for a strictly uniform conception of independent study. Nevertheless the long history of negotiation and compromise between the senate and the independent studies group without doubt increased the ambiguities which surrounded the school from its inception. The limitations of resource, the restriction on the number of full-time staff, and the political vulnerability of the whole scheme demonstrably retarded the removal of those ambiguities.

The 1975/76 prospectus of the school stated its aims in only the very vaguest of terms:

'. . . planning their own schemes of study, students have the opportunity to orient their learning to achieve their own goals, to examine problems relevant to their own experience and interests and to understand and evaluate the learning process.'

The regulations of the school, provided and required by senate, do, by implication, place an emphasis on the written work, which is presented in the third year, as the overall goal. The structure of assessment and concern with comparability of standards emphasize the same goal. The crucial issue for the school that arises both from this study and from a consideration of the school's history is whether it has succeeded in striking the right balance between a concern for the development of self-directed learning for individual students and a determination to assuage the legitimate anxieties of the university that what is done is academically worthwhile and not alien from the activities of the academic environment which surrounds it.

A lack of clarity and agreement about their role and activities was very apparent in interviews with directors of study. The clear statement about a developmental learning process for students and the related role of staff of the 1972 discussion document (quoted above, page 35) had clearly not been translated into the practice of the school in 1974/76. No doubt this fact can be attributed, in part, to the limited resources allocated to the school and to the voluntary nature of the directors' involvement, but it is not clear that the educational philosophies of the early full-time staff necessarily led them to all of the same conclusions as the planning group.

In fact, when asked why they had volunteered to supervise independent studies students only five of the twelve part-time directors of study interviewed gave answers which showed that they had any perception of what the general purpose of an independent studies scheme might be. All five of these had been involved in the original deliberations on the subject. The remaining seven gave interesting but diverse reasons for their involvement. One said that with 'the course structure as it is people don't get enough opportunity to specialize in one area. I think it is better for a student to know something in depth than it is to get general knowledge. This is the important one and the one which induced me to teach in this context.' Another admitted that she 'didn't know much about the school' but agreed to supervise because a student had approached her. Another felt that the brighter students 'gravitated towards independent study' and that they 'were not typical of the under-graduate school as a whole, they were more mature' and he wanted the opportunity to teach the students although he had 'misgivings as to the academic sense of having undergraduates study by themselves'. A senior member wanted more inter-disciplinary study because 'my own interest is broader than one department', while another was interested in 'supervising students in my particular area'.

With these diverse reasons—some with a concern for specialization, and others for the teaching of brighter students—thus reflecting a spirit contrary to that of the original scheme, it was not surprising that the aims of some of the directors of studies clashed with those of their students, sometimes with what may be perceived as unfortunate results. One of the most serious issues—as described by students—was the inability of some directors to see beyond the confines of their disciplines so that they approached the student and his project from a strictly specialist standpoint. One student expressed this strongly, observing that 'lecturers are slaves of their disciplines, they see things in terms of the discipline and not the wider view'. And some of the directors had no sense of commitment at all to independent studies as a concept, or as an area of the university, and were unlikely to develop one. As one of the full-time staff members of the school put it, 'some directors of studies don't have much contact with the school, some don't want any contact'.

By contrast the students almost unanimously had a definite area of interest which they wanted to pursue, free from the confines of departments and—if necessary—from particular disciplines. Most of them expressed dissatisfaction and dis-illusionment with the coursework and methods of teaching during their first year at university. One student spoke on behalf of several of his colleagues when he said that 'the value of independent studies is the goal and not the grade', while another said 'the very process of being extended gives you a feeling of satisfaction'. Another student summed up what many felt when he stated, 'I am not that interested in the end product because I hope to do this study for years more. Therefore I am interested in the processes that have got me to this stage.' Indeed, among the students was a classic example of an autodidact, of a mature student who had worked in a number of jobs and travelled the world, and developed an interest in a particularly complex field of study (international security and strategic studies) which he had pursued independently of conventional educational institutions for about ten years. He had come to Lancaster specifically to work in the School of Independent Studies. He finally achieved a 2(i) and was accepted at another university for postgraduate research in his chosen field.

Yet even the most independent and single-minded of students emphasized how crucial was a good working relationship with the director of studies and how potentially disastrous it would be if director and student could not agree on the orientation of the work. One student commented 'you're working so closely with one lecturer that if there is poor rapport, you're really in a bad situation for four terms'. At least five of the students interviewed had experienced a breakdown in the relationship with their director of studies. One described a situation in which:

'I have had very little or no help or contact from my supervisor for the last year. It wasn't due to a personality clash. It had a lot to do with the way I approached my work. It was a matter of different perceptions . . .'

His director of studies, said the student, was out of sympathy with his own 'theoretical' approach: 'He has never fully understood what I was trying to do and he tried to direct into areas I didn't want to go.' Such an intellectual conflict might have been educationally very fruitful, but there were pedagogic weaknesses too. The student recalled that: 'We never sat down together to talk over the topic. He never questioned my assumptions at the beginning, he just accepted it.' This student said that working completely on his own 'didn't bother' him. However, when the time came for his work to be submitted much of it was hurried and more limited in scope than his original proposal. He graduated with a 2(ii).

One director of studies supervised a number of independent student majors, one of whom reported that his director had been of only limited use to him:

'He is interested and he will help you. He has difficulty in supervising my topic. The narrowness of the field of academic staff will result in the director of studies not being able to advise you adequately. We have different perceptions of the work. His approach is different to mine. He is a politician, I am a historian. I only see him when I need to. I don't come out of his sessions inspired.'

But another student, supervised by the same man, reflected on a very successful relationship:

'My supervisor is exactly as I would like my supervisor to be. He doesn't breathe down my neck. He is not an expert in the subject but intellectually he is as sharp as a razor. I can bounce things off him, but it comes straight back. His comments and corrections to my work are excellent.'

Some directors of studies found that when the students first approached them they were very vague about the area they wanted to study and the form the project would take. This early stage was the most difficult for a director. The problem as they saw it was to judge how far the director *should* try to restructure his student's project without interfering with the independence of the student. What was the correct balance between help and independence? And, anyway, as one director admitted, 'I don't know how you define dependence in education'. A director, after pointing out the difficulties involved, was definite about the course directors should take:

'Supervisors should tread fairly carefully, they don't want to let rubbish go through, but on the other hand their role in telling the student what to say is a difficult one; they can't write the thesis for the student. They can't ignore what the student has written . . . for the undergraduate one has no misgivings about identifying the weak spots.'

The fact that the director is dealing with undergraduates makes his task much more difficult because many of the students have limited experience with academic work and in some cases limited background preparation for the chosen project. One director observed: 'The more you minimize the student's lack of background the more you interfere with the scheme.' The fact that a large number of independent studies students are mature students appeared to increase the problems in this early period because, said some directors, mature students have more fixed ideas which are harder to change.

It was clear that students wanted more than an occasional meeting with their directors, more than intermittent pieces of guidance and feedback. They felt that it was essential that a bond—both academic and personal—ought to grow between a director and a student, because independent studies students, particularly, needed someone who would provide a sense of security and belonging to compensate for the amorphous nature of the school. Not all directors recognized or accepted this need. One student who did not enjoy rapport with his director suggested that:

'. . . there must be a close personal relationship; the director of study must be really interested in the student's work and through working together a bond grows between them.'

A majority of the students interviewed said that studying independently had decreased their contact with other students and lecturers and a number claimed that independent study had increased rather than decreased anxiety and nervous strain. They felt that directors could help to relieve anxiety by encouragement and guidance. In particular, they needed to know whether they were progressing satisfactorily, and would meet the required standard. If criticism had to be made, said students, it should be made in the awareness that for many independent studies students a special relationship existed between the student and his work. He became emotionally involved in what he was doing and the project became one of the most important aspects of his life for a long period. A member of the full-time staff of the school reflected on the dangers of de-motivating a student by non-constructive criticism: 'You are attacking a whole person's being and therefore it has to be constructive to be acceptable.'

It was ironic that in this School of Independent Studies one of the factors which most worried students, and most bemused directors, was the system of final grading and assessment. The fears of the original planning group that grading would distort the philosophy of self-directed learning appeared to be justified. It was mainly the uncertainty of the assessment procedures that caused student anxiety: the absence of explicitly stated objectives and criteria. They did not know how their work was going to be marked. At least conventional students could look up past years' examination papers. One independent studies student commented:

> 'I find it difficult not exactly knowing who one is aiming at or the volume of work required. I am worried that any work will be assessed in terms of PhD work and standard.'

It was a common fear among these students that since they were generally believed to be a more highly-motivated group, and in some ways were specially privileged, their work would be expected to be of 'higher quality and depth' than that of other undergraduates. They also reported a body of opinion amongst themselves (which was mistaken, according to official sources) 'which says you are doing six units so you must produce 100,000 words, six units worth.' Indeed, one of the full-time staff members of the school observed that some of the directors of study appeared to be looking for 'postgraduate quality and undergraduate quantity'. One student concluded 'somehow you can't know which to aim at—probably both'.

The division of work into units, and the necessity of allocating different weightings to different pieces of work, was—in the view of most students and many staff—'an unnecessary hassle'. One student described how he had felt obliged to manipulate the weightings of.his work when it came to the final assessment:

> 'I realized that the scheme was devised because people are preoccupied with issuing pieces of paper. I was unhappy to divide up my work because I wanted someone to read the whole project and see lines of development. The weighting I came to in the end was internally political. Because I felt the external examiner would not appreciate two areas I weighted these down although a great deal of work had gone into them. Two other areas I weighted up because I knew they would be more acceptable although I knew the quality wasn't as good.'

Students and directors were asked in what ways they believed students in the school were, and should be, 'independent'. The answers revealed differences of opinion between the two groups. Many of the students talked of independence in terms of 'just doing my own thing', 'having absolute freedom', and suggested that they were really independent with regard to the choice of topic, the choice of method of assessment, the timing of the project and the form of presentation. By contrast, lecturers felt that there was a pattern of oscillation between dependence and independence that was common to most students. They agreed that students were at their most independent early in their programme of work but this changed to dependence as they prepared to submit their work. Many directors felt that this situation was wrong in a scheme in which students ought to become progressively more independent. The pressures of putting the final submission into shape and the anxieties about the quality of the work led students at the end of their degree to rely too heavily on the director's judgement and guidance. He, after all, was one of the examiners.

The Structure of the School of Independent Studies

At the time of the research, the school had only two full-time members of staff. The supervision of students was mainly undertaken, in addition to their normal teaching commitment, by members of existing teaching departments, acting voluntarily. The result was that the central activities of the school were minimal and of an administrative nature, and that academic interaction and discussion was almost exclusively between student and director of studies—with limited feedback to the school. The school had little coherence as an academic entity in its own right.

For some students this situation was as they wanted it; they were not 'interested in the school as a structure'. Others were concerned that independent study also implied isolation:

'. . . independent studies cuts you off from your friends. You can't really communicate with them intellectually as they don't know enough about what you are doing—you are on your own.'

One student was concerned that in the school there was not an 'awareness of the emotional aspect . . . this aspect could get lost and people will be told to produce good pieces of academic work' and nothing else. He meant that students needed to be treated as individuals, that independent studies caused particular problems, and that it was important that there should be some safety net which ensured that these problems were dealt with sympathetically. Several of the students felt very strongly about their academic isolation; they, above all, were concerned with more than just achieving a high degree classification and yet they were cut off from a sense of academic community.

Some directors of study felt, too, that they would benefit from the existence of a more corporate structure in the school. One of the original aims of the independent studies planning group had been to introduce a means of cross-departmental and divergent educational thinking into the university. One of the directors commented: 'The school is potentially a focus of intellectual discussion between members of different departments which doesn't naturally exist.' But there were other directors who, more pragmatically, wanted the school to have a real existence in helping them to be successful supervisors of independent studies students. Those who were directors for the first time looked for advice on their role, on the degrees of independence to allow the student, on how to guide a student in drawing up his scheme of assessed units of work, on how often to see the student. There were information sheets from the school but these went only part of the way towards meeting the apparent needs for guidance of some directors.

NOTES

[1] The whole of this chapter is based on Lewin (1976).

[2] Unattributed quotations in the following paragraphs come from early discussion documents of the group.

[3] The outline of the School of Independent Studies in this section largely describes it as it was first established in 1973/4. Variations and developments are referred to in Chapter 4 and Postscript 2.

[4] The school was established with four categories of staff:
  i the director;
  ii full-time staff (only one was appointed in 1973/4);
  iii staff who assist with independent studies on a part time basis, but the extent of whose involvement requires a diminution of their normal teaching load (so called category (b) staff—none has so far been appointed);
  iv staff who assist with independent studies on a part-time basis, without any diminution of their normal teaching load, and to an extent not exceeding 20 per cent of their normal teaching load (from this category directors of studies are normally drawn).

[5] The Committee for Independent Studies consists of the full-time staff of the school, senate-appointed members and elected representatives of the directors of studies. For non-reserved business (ie excluding matters of the approval and assessment of schemes of study) elected representatives of independent studies students are members.

[6] The main external examiner also scrutinized schemes of study.

[7] Since 1975 students have been able to apply through the Universities Central Council on Admissions to take independent studies at Lancaster. They take a normal three-subject Part 1 course and are required to prepare a substantial submission in the same way as other students, before proceeding to Part 2 independent studies. To date, only a small number of students have applied for independent studies through UCCA.

[8] Comments by individuals in this section are drawn from interviews by John Lewin in his evaluatory study in 1976. See pages 40–50 of this chapter.

[9] In the spring and summer of 1976 John Lewin interviewed ten out of the fourteen independent studies students who were to graduate in 1976 (8 majors and 2 minors). He also interviewed twelve directors of studies representing all departments in the school, present and former full-time staff of the school and other senior members of the university. Throughout he used an open-ended interview schedule. He also corresponded with the external examiner of the school. The material in this section is largely based on his study. In the summer of 1975, Duncan Nimmo interviewed—as a preliminary investigation—four out of the six independent studies majors graduating that year. Extracts from these interviews were also used in writing this section.

CHANGES IN INDEPENDENT STUDY AT NELP SINCE 1976

Substantial revisions have been made to the structure of the NELP DipHE since the research reported in Chapter 2 of this book was carried out. The School for Independent Study has also begun to operate a part-time DipHE and a degree by independent study. The part-time course started in April 1977; the degree course in September 1976.

The Full-time DipHE

After the first diplomates had graduated in June 1976 the school took stock of its position in a document (NELP 1976) summarizing the experiences of the previous two years and outlining proposals for the future. Careful note was taken of observations made by tutors, students, examiners, visitors to the school, and of the report made to the course group on which Chapter 2 is based. The school had earlier stated that its work should be exposed to the maximum external criticism, and the organizers of the DipHE were ready to admit errors:

> '. . . we have encouraged comment, carefully collated submitted criticism, and have sought explicitly to use our failures as a basis for further improvement . . . Throughout the past two years we have been clear in our own minds that because no-one had previously worked on a programme of this nature we would make mistakes. We have made mistakes, some of them major . . .'
>
> (NELP 1976)

The principal changes instituted since 1976 are in assessment, the planning period, the objectives of the course, and the organization of group and individual work—particularly central studies work. There have been compromises on the originally extensive amount of freedom given to students and much more structure, especially in the early stages of the course, is now provided. The programme has tried to make its own aims more explicit. What was previously a 'hidden curriculum' of expected general aims—never made clear to students, but nevertheless a condition for success—has now been formalized as a list of objectives required by the nature of the programme for all students. For example, all students are now expected to demonstrate an ability to 'work with people and on projects not directly related to their own individual expertise'. A more recent DipHE prospectus (NELP 1977) explains the rationale behind independent study, makes clearer the role of teacher and student in such a context, and defines more extensively the notions of competence, independence and interdependence, and transferability of skills. The difficulties facing prospective students are outlined (cf the comments of the first DipHE students, pages 21–23 above), and it is made apparent that the course will not suit all students —in spite of the 'flexible entry policy' of the school and of the polytechnic. 'Independent study can be tough', warns the prospectus; '. . . the course is quite definitely *not* for someone who really wants a traditionally-structured course, but cannot get on one due to lack of 'A' levels'. Presumably, this policy is also now reflected in the selection of students.

The preparatory planning period at the beginning of the course of study has itself been much altered. The aim of drawing up a contract containing statements of objectives and the means of assessing them, which is then submitted to the validating board for approval, remains. But the planning period is now longer and students are more dependent on their tutors during it. The first three weeks are an introductory phase; students make tentative statements of aims. From the end of October to February students are introduced to the theory and practice of a range of transferable skills in workshops, seminars, and projects, all led by tutors. These units include the planning of projects, information retrieval, and research methods in arts, social science, and natural science. An important criticism made by the external examiners who assessed the first DipHE students was the methodological weakness of group project activities, and these units are designed to help remedy such a deficiency. During this time students also discuss initial plans for individual work with staff from an appropriate faculty of the polytechnic, and students have a trial attachment with a tutor. At the beginning of the second term the individual tutor, the student's personal tutor from the school, and the student meet to discuss the relationship of the proposed individual work to the student's objectives. At the end of February the student's proposals are submitted for validation.

After the planning period, students are expected to continue to follow group work 'back-up units' related to their own objectives, although the projects they then participate in are no longer directly linked to the units. Students are now required to participate in a fixed number of group projects each term. There have been no major changes in the operation of individual work (previously called special interest work) after the planning period, although the increased help given in movement into faculties during the period has helped to meet the early student criticisms of poor liaison between the school and the faculties.

One of the failings of the programme in its original form was a lack of clarity about assessment procedures and an inadequate amount of feedback on student performance in group work. Since the first terminal assessment took place in 1976 the details of its actual operation can now be made clearer to present students; neither staff nor students knew what to expect in 1974/76. A formalization of the diagnostic assessment procedures for group work has also been made. Written and verbal assessments of any group project that lasts longer than four weeks are now given to project groups by a panel consisting of the project tutor, two other members of staff, and a student representative.

Other changes to the programme in response to criticisms include a reorganization of staff responsibilities in the school to permit more effective control over problem areas such as central studies work, more opportunities for student feedback on the operation of the programme, and the establishment of procedures to enable closer liaison between external examiners and the validating board. The extent to which these and the other changes outlined have been effective is not easy to judge. There is a need for further evaluation of the programme by external observers, possibly along the lines of the 1975/76 evaluatory studies, before one can be certain that the difficulties then identified have been overcome.

The Degree by Independent Study

In February 1976 the school submitted proposals to the CNAA for a new course leading to the award of a degree by independent study. The course was approved in July 1976, in time for the first entrants—who were required as a condition of the approval to be NELP DipHE graduates—to begin the course that year. Twelve students enrolled in September; because the degree allows termly entry, four others joined it in January 1977.

The justification for the degree arose from the polytechnic's commitment to provide post-diploma opportunities for DipHE graduates. A built-in tension developed between, on the one hand, the school's desire to define the diploma as a qualification in its own right, and, on the other, the commitment to provide further courses and the understandable 'drift' of students towards the desire for a degree qualification. The original idea that diplomates might be admitted to the third year of conventional polytechnic courses was in many cases acceptable in principle to the faculties but was thought to be impractical. Consequently, students wishing to proceed with further study after obtaining the DipHE in 1976 were effectively faced with the alternative of entering a degree course at the polytechnic or elsewhere at first- or second-year level (and four of the first diplomates did this), or with submitting programme proposals for a degree by independent study. All diplomates possessed a right to the latter option. About two-thirds of the submitted proposals were accepted.

The submission for the degree[1] drew upon the experiences of the first two years of the DipHE programme and attempted to adapt the 'polytechnic philosophy' (see above, pages 10–11) to third-year degree level work. The rationale for the degree leaned heavily on the ideas of the 'new' sociology of education (see, for example, Young 1971; and for a summary and critique, Karabel and Halsey 1977); in particular, the proposal was concerned that 'educational knowledge' should not be synonymous with 'valid knowledge'. If curricula are defined, in Young's (1971) terms, as expressions of the principles governing the organization and selection of knowledge, then the designers of the NELP degree desired that the dominant forms of organization and selection expressed by the course structure should not be those of 'educators' but rather those of 'citizens'. The egalitarian appeal of the underlying relativism of the 'new' sociology of education fitted the NELP educational philosophy closely; once again, the structure of an independent study programme was seen as the logical means of implementing the philosophy. This time, however, the connection was expressed in the language of sociology:

'The implication of our situation must be that we cannot present ourselves as the controllers of an autonomous educational system but instead as components of the social system involved with students in defining the meaning and purpose of the educational sub-system . . . the programmes of study devised by students should be devised by citizens in negotiation with citizens rather than by the educated in negotiation with educators.'

(NELP 1978)

The original submission stressed the need to define a clear boundary between the roles of teacher and student. Students are expected to define their own programmes of study within a non-negotiable course structure defined by staff. This structure includes a compulsory 'pre-course' during which students submit their proposals for their programmes to a registration board, the statement including required paragraphs on the style of study to be used, the intellectual justification for the programme, and the proposed methods of assessment. Students are also required to name two referees. Students are obliged, once the proposal has been accepted, to keep to the forms of specialist tutor contact and attendance which they have specified, and to adhere strictly to the assessment methods proposed. A rigorous specification of methods and objectives is expected. The process of registration was a protracted one in the original submission, and the re-submission made it even more so; in the new structure, the 'pre-course' is a part-time evening or correspondence course lasting an entire year. Draft proposals are made in the second term, after students have spent the first working through a series of tasks concentrating on the analysis and description of their previous higher education course. The proposals are then referred to faculty sub-boards of the registration board; the sub-boards refer the students to appropriate specialist tutors; definitive proposals are submitted in the third term. Recommendations for the award of the degree are made by an assessment board consisting of a specialist tutor, representatives of all the polytechnic faculties, and external examiners, after consideration of the products of each student's work.

The students' programmes have, in practice, largely been ones of individual work, although it is possible for them to submit proposals based on group activities. The re-submission of the degree proposal to the CNAA asserts that 'students generally should be given the opportunity, in the third year of their undergraduate education, to design their own programmes of study', and suggests that by 1980 students from other courses at NELP and students from DipHE courses elsewhere should be admitted. It is significant that a clear concern 'to safeguard the standard of the degrees recommended by the polytechnic under the title of independent study' and for the 'rigour of methods' informs the new submission. The contrast between it and the original DipHE submission is considerable in this respect.

The Part-time DipHE

The part-time DipHE course follows closely the principles of the full-time programme, and accords with the NELP commitment to the provision of opportunities for local students and for those who do not come straight from school. The course takes a minimum of three years to complete. It begins with a residential weekend as the first part of the planning period. The chief differences between the part-time and the full-time courses are in the teaching arrangements.

Students are members of 'sets' of about five plus a school tutor. The sets meet weekly, and provide the main focus of support for students; they replace the full-time DipHE central studies projects. The reasoning behind the set system appears to derive from the characteristics of the facilitative and acceptant groups used in Rogerian therapy and learning. The tutor acts as facilitator, never leader; the set is intended to offer a supportive environment in which students can participate responsibly in learning without threat to their self-images; students are expected to learn 'real-life' transferable social skills in the groups.

One evening each week is set aside as a 'core evening'. All students are required to attend to ensure that they meet each other regularly. The time is used to give information about course administration, for lectures by polytechnic staff from other faculties, for careers discussions, for group exercises in learning problems and study skills, and for student seminars on areas of common concern.

Individual work arrangements are similar to those for the full-time DipHE, although the times available for consultation between individual tutors and students are naturally more constrained.

CHANGES IN INDEPENDENT STUDIES AT LANCASTER SINCE 1976

The independent studies scheme at Lancaster has undergone a variety of changes since 1975/76. The number of full-time staff in the school has increased to four (three academic and one administrative). Thus the school's potential for organizing central activities and supervising students has increased. However, each of the four staff is involved in teaching part-time for other departments in the university—this development being partly the result of quid pro quo arrangements which made the appointment of the additional staff possible. Indeed, the period of the school's development has coincided throughout with the most difficult years of the University of Lancaster since its inception. Inflation, financial restraint and limited growth created an atmosphere in the university in which, in one interpretation, the School of Independent Studies would be fortunate to survive, but certainly could not attempt to develop according to the ideals of its originators. The opponents of the independent studies scheme did not disappear merely because the senate had voted it into experimental existence.

The number of major students in the school has stabilized at about 15 each year, with roughly the same number of minors. However, the number of provisional registrations has greatly increased, to over a hundred per year. It is clear that many students are registering without the intention of doing more than their Free Ninth

Unit in independent studies; they have a special interest but they only wish to spend a small section of their Part 2 course on it. On the other hand, the record shows that there is considerable 'switching' behaviour among students once provisionally registered—from major to minor, from Free Ninth to major, etc. It is now possible for students who are well advanced with their plans to have their major or minor submissions approved at the start of the second year and about half of the major students do so.

The full-time staff of the school have extended their activities by attempting to give the school more of a communal identity, by increasing their guidance of directors of study, and by asking for more feedback on students' progress. A school assembly meets regularly and all students, directors and full-time staff are eligible to attend. The assembly is advisory in nature, discusses university and school matters, and elects a different chairman for each meeting. A regular newsletter is sent out with reminders about deadlines and procedures for submission and assessment, and with advice on study skills and problems. Series of general seminars, led by either students or staff, are organized on specialist topics or on issues related to independent studies. Directors of study are asked to complete regular report forms on their students, and students are invited to meet a nominated member of the central staff at intervals to discuss progress. The director of the school now writes a general letter of guidance to directors of studies.

The academic year 1976/77 was duly determined by the original senate in 1973 to be the year for a review of whether the School of Independent Studies should continue beyond the experimental period. A small senate sub-committee was established in the Lent term of 1977. After taking views and evidence from a wide range of interested parties, the sub-committee recommended to senate in March 1977 that the school's 'existence should be confirmed as an established part of the university'. The sub-committee noted that all the opinions it had received were uniformly in favour of the school and 'we ourselves were convinced of the value and academic justification of its activity' (Lancaster University Senate 1977). Few, if any, voices were raised in dissent and senate agreed to the recommendation without hesitation. It was a measure of the considerable national and international interest which the school had excited since 1973 and of its value as a very evident symbol of the university's continuing innovative nature. It was, too, a measure of the political success of the school and its full-time staff in surviving in a sometimes hostile environment, and of the durability of the compromises enforced on the original independent studies group in 1972/3. In particular, the Committee of Independent Studies had come to act as a protector and protagonist of the school, while maintaining its original role of senate's watchdog over the scheme.

In May 1977, the sub-committee reported again to senate, as required, on a number of questions connected with the operation of the independent studies scheme.[2] Interestingly, they observed that 'students have somewhat different ideas about the meaning of "independent"' and 'we ourselves have not been able to agree on a clear definition'. Among the sub-committee's major recommendations were the suggestion that the possibility of appointing some Category (b) staff (see page 50) should be examined; that in particular cases students (probably mature students) should be enabled to take all nine units of Part 2 in independent studies; that there should not be a Part 1 course in independent studies although some group seminars and discussions at that stage would be desirable; that major students should have more than one director of studies; that there should be much more group work and meetings among students to create a sense of community (although the sub-committee reported that the students it saw 'expressed little interest in such developments and were, on the whole, doubtful whether a sufficient community of interest existed to provide a basis for sustained joint activities'); that directors of studies should be offered more guidance by the school; that in particular cases earlier and staggered submission of work to be assessed should be encouraged from students; that all major students should have an automatic viva voce examination on their work (Lancaster University Senate 1977).

For a variety of reasons many of these recommendations—particularly those implying an increase of staff resources—have not been acted upon by the university. There are unlikely to be viva voce examinations, or early submissions of work in the School of Independent Studies. It is not likely that a nine-unit Part 2 course, or a Part 1 course, in independent studies will be possible. But undoubtedly the sub-committee report was a boost to the morale of the school and its permanent establishment removed the uncertainties. It was in July 1977, in fact, that the third member of the full-time staff took up his post. The school is proceeding cautiously to offer more guidance to directors of studies and students, to ensure that each student's progress is known, and to encourage students to engage in group activity. In 1979 a residential study weekend was held.

SOME COMMENTS ON THE NELP AND LANCASTER SCHEMES OF INDEPENDENT STUDY

It is difficult not to be aware of the common features and conclusions of these two case studies in independent study at NELP and Lancaster, despite the evident differences in the schemes and the contexts in which they were conceived and have operated. We think that they provide useful indicators for future attempts to introduce comprehensive schemes of independent study into British universities and polytechnics, and, more generally, they throw light on the fate of radical attempts to innovate in higher education.

There can be no doubt that both schemes were far-reaching in intent. They originated in deep-seated reaction to current courses of higher education; their supporters rejected conventional planning, structure, and organization in favour of an emphasis on individuality and spontaneity. The philosophy of independent study emphasizes the need for the student to develop his own sense of direction, to follow a growing awareness of self that might lead to any point of the intellectual or emotional compass. One of our conclusions is that independent study schemes carry in them a logic that, if it is taken as too universal, too homogeneous, will adopt a model of the student that is just as rigid, just as unreal as that of conventional courses. Conventional courses could be characterized as assuming a 'greenhouse concept' of the student: he is placed in a protected environment, in a hothouse removed from the everyday world; he is to be watered with well-established teaching methods and fed on the intellectual resources of books and libraries; if all goes well he will grow—despite himself. Independent study programmes may make parallel assumptions, which we could characterize as the 'Robinson Crusoe concept' of the student: he is washed up on the intellectual shore; he has around him the resources he needs; and in him (lying dormant but ready to be awakened), the skills and motivations necessary for him to recreate a personally relevant culture; if he fends actively for himself he will survive; if he survives he will be a different person. Yet it is certainly clear that not all students are Robinson Crusoes, even if they want to be. Some might survive and prosper on the desert island if they had the opportunity to retreat to the greenhouse for intervals of recuperation. Others might find that they could be Robinson Crusoes only for short periods of the year.

It was evident in the independent study schools both at Lancaster and NELP that some students coped better than others with their freedom and unusual circumstances. At Lancaster this was implicitly recognized by the stringent screening-out and admissions procedure; at NELP the more open admissions policy was matched by a high student drop-out rate. Indeed, as suggested in Chapter 1, one could predict from the research into differences between students that some students would not adapt successfully to the absence of structure which independent study implies. It is possible to conclude from the later developments at Lancaster and NELP reported earlier in this chapter that there has been a movement from the early primitive emphasis on spontaneity and pragmatism in independent study schemes to a more overt awareness of a need for structure and common practice. This should not be seen as a betrayal of the faith of the planning group at Lancaster and the working group at NELP, nor as inevitable institutionalized routinization or bureaucratization. Rather it is a recognition of weaknesses in the original schemes and of the experiences of students in the schemes. It is true, additionally, that reports of the two evaluatory studies described in this book were made available to the full-time staff of the two schools. At NELP, in particular, the findings were partially responsible for subsequent changes.

Whatever their hopes and convictions, students who enter Lancaster University and NELP are not born anew. They come with many years' experience of pedagogic situations in which there are a teacher to whom questions can be addressed, a recognizable body of knowledge to be assimilated, and tests, examinations and prizes as measurements of progress. It takes elements of determination and courage to break away from this predictable and comfortable learning environment to enrol in a course of independent study. However motivated or experienced a student might be, a programme of independent study can be fraught with unpredicted problems and inevitable anxieties. The screening and admission procedure at Lancaster did not produce students who were untouched by such anxieties; indeed, it is not clear that it was trying (or should have been trying) to do so. Nor is there any easy, one-to-one correspondence between 'maturity' and 'independence'. Mature students (who, we have noted, were particularly attracted to both schemes) often have additional, well-recognized difficulties: with study skills, in their lack of academic background, and with overconfidence. We think that these phenomena are well exemplified in the case studies of Chapters 2 and 3 and that the movements towards greater structure and co-ordination at NELP and Lancaster are wise responses to early problems.

The Lancaster and NELP schemes depended for their existence on the involvement of a broad range of staff from their respective institutions, who tutored students on a part-time basis. We found it notable that among these staff there were such differing conceptions of their roles and of the degree and kind of help and guidance that they should give to independent study students.

At NELP there were staff with radically different philosophies—those who perceived independent study as concerned with 'new' higher education goals of growth and the development of sensitivity and feeling, and others who were concerned that the departure from the canons of rationality and intellectualism might be too radical and too far-reaching. At Lancaster there were some directors of studies who wished to see intellectual growth in the student that would take him across the boundaries of disciplines and departments to a concept of the whole university as a resource, and others who regarded themselves as directing a student on a specialist topic in a similar relationship to that of supervisor and research student. At NELP it was the case that there was a strongly expressed but generalized and inchoate school philosophy from which some staff dissented in part; at Lancaster there was no coherent philosophy—rather a careful academic pragmatism that was heir to the uneasy concordat worked out between planning group and senate. At Lancaster directors of studies made of the situation what they could.

Did it matter? It meant that some students at both institutions found themselves frustrated by their relative deprivation compared with other independent study students. Some central studies groups at NELP felt that their time was being wasted while other groups were engaged in worthwhile projects. Students at Lancaster who had not established a fruitful relationship with their own director of studies observed fellow students enjoying a mutually beneficial intellectual and personal dialogue with their directors. It was possible for a tutor at NELP to define any experience—no matter how apparently frustrating or unsatisfactory for the student—as 'growth', 'learning', 'development'. It was feasible for a Lancaster director of studies to argue that he was misnamed: he should 'direct' nothing, he was there as a resource (indeed, a volunteer resource) for an independent study student to use, or not use, as he would. Students at both institutions needed a high degree of self-confidence and a strong sense of direction to be able to tolerate the conflicting definitions of the situation and modes of operation among staff.

In fact, we would argue—on the basis of the student interviews—that it is expecting too much of most students to admit them directly into the context of independent study without some form of preparation. Certainly Lancaster students had greater chances of coping because they entered independent study in their second year of higher education and, for a time, most had both conventional courses and preparatory work for independent study running side-by-side; at NELP the student (including the unconventionally qualified mature student) found himself involved in independent study from the start of his experience of higher education. On the other hand, the NELP School for Independent Study developed a comprehensive preparatory and planning period in which students began to assess their own competences and to set objectives (and the appropriate modes of assessment) for themselves. In an ideal scheme of independent study, it seems to us, students would be admitted after some experience of conventional courses and would attempt to diagnose their own weaknesses and strengths as students, would work on study skills and familiarize themselves with the total resources that their institution and its neighbourhood might offer them. It would be useful for students to try to define the objectives they would wish to achieve through independent study—objectives relating to skills, abilities and attitudes as well as to knowledge areas.

It is possible to argue that a scheme of independent study which requires tutors and students to work in similar ways, to move in the same direction, and to accept forms of centralized structure and feedback, is illogical. The essence of independence might be its unpredictability: that student and tutor should be free to establish whatever learning relationship is the most fruitful for them. Additionally— particularly at Lancaster where the school depended entirely on the goodwill of the volunteer directors of studies for whom every student was an addition to their teaching load—it could reasonably be claimed that staff could in no way be required to have common ways of working. But the two evaluatory studies have convinced us that if independent study schemes are not to be confined to the most able and self-reliant students, then there must be systems of back-up support for students and guidance on 'good practice' for staff. Such developments are easier to visualize within a scheme based on Dressel and Thompson's notion of independent study as an academic competence to be developed, rather than within a humanistic/ psychological conception of independent study drawn from models of client-orientated therapy. The implication for schemes of independent study is not, of course, the drafting of hierarchical sequences of behavioural objectives, but rather an affirmation that each student will develop, and be seen to develop, the skills and attitudes of independent learning during his programme of study. We would like to see a broad line of development in the relationship between student and tutor/ director of studies: a movement from a degree of student dependence to relative independence; a shift in the source of ideas, guidance and initiatives from tutor to student. In order to achieve this there would have to be a more common approach and attitude to their role among all the tutors/directors of studies drawn from different parts of the institution; co-ordination by the central staff; and some kind of preparatory or induction programme for new directors of study. But a very delicate balance has to be established between planning and structure on the one hand and freedom and spontaneity on the other, and it is on this issue that the NELP and

Lancaster schemes are still feeling their way. What we are sure about, however, is that, in practice, the prevalence of the 'ideal-type' of student/tutor relationship— of the highly-motivated committed student working out a confident academic destiny in equal dialogue with a conscientious, facilitating tutor—cannot be assumed in any scheme of independent study. The interest and the motivation may be present in both parties, but the conditions and context of a positive, developing tutorial relationship have to be planned for and fostered.

We have shown clearly that a further fundamental idea lying behind the two independent study schemes was the wish to counteract perceived trends towards large, undifferentiated institutions of higher education and depersonalized teaching situations by emphasizing learning which was personally relevant, taking place in a supportive, like-minded community. Yet the feelings of isolation which independent study students in both institutions experienced were well-documented in Chapters 2 and 3. At Lancaster they probably ceased attending any lectures or seminars in their last four terms; students reported their sense of loneliness even in residence on campus because fellow students could not, or would not, talk to them about their work. And yet the independent study student was, above all, likely to want to discuss work because, for him, it was closer to the surface, more central to his self-definition.

It does seem that there are real issues here for independent study schemes. By entering one of the schools the student was setting himself apart from conventional and safe modes of studying (and, probably, reducing the number of 'formal' contact hours and range of staff contact that a conventional course would have provided). He was also putting himself in a situation where he could not so easily identify with a group of peers, where he could not easily share his anxieties. Should a school attempt to create such a group for the student? The approach in NELP and Lancaster proved to be different. At Lancaster, students of independent studies have never been required as a condition of studying within the school to meet in groups and work together on projects. In contrast, the NELP school emphasized interdependent as well as independent study; a conscious attempt was made to foster a variety of interpersonal and social skills and to reduce the isolation of the independent study student by requiring him to participate in group work. As we have seen, however, this did not guarantee immunity from anxieties and insecurities related to a perceived absence of common goals. In the early years, moreover, some students felt that group work was a hindrance to their academic progress, because their own interests were so different from those of their colleagues.

At NELP, the school was physically isolated: to an extent this was a matter of policy as well as of necessity. In the conception of some of its protagonists, the NELP school was to be the seedcorn of radical change in higher education. It had to be kept intact from contamination by the remainder of the institution. Indeed, both schools were the object of suspicion, if not of opposition, from certain parts of their host institution. At NELP it seems that the school developed a sense of community and, with its generalized radical philosophy, was an entity with which the student could, if he wished, identify. But, of course, a sense of community is possible without a philosophy, radical or otherwise: it can be based on common problems and experiences and on similarity of intellectual concerns. At Lancaster in the early years the situation was difficult: the school had few full-time staff, not much of a physical identity and little reason for meeting as a community. It was perceived only as an administrative necessity; directors of studies felt loyalty to their students rather than to the school. The rationale behind some of the changes in the Lancaster scheme in recent years has, of course, been that of developing just this sense of community. But, as we noted earlier, Lancaster independent study students commented to the senate sub-committee in 1977 that their interests were too dissimilar for such attempts at fostering an artificial community to succeed.

A crucial area of similarity between the two case studies relates to problems of assessment. In both schemes students were worried about assessment, about the 'standard' that was required and how the quality of their work related to it, about the form it would take and how necessary it was for them to fit their work to pre-conceived models. No doubt all students worry about assessment, but the anxiety was particularly acute for independent study students at both institutions. Here, particularly, they perceived themselves as in a situation of high risk: there were no easy precedents for them to follow and certainly no past examination papers for them to look at. At Lancaster there were all the problems over weighting and the rush to complete an 'acceptable' quantity of written work by the due date. At NELP there was the special final group exercise in which there were uncertainties about the criteria by which each individual would be judged and the complexities of fitting the final presentation of special interest written work to the varied and uneven objectives pre-set by the individual student. To an extent, for all students, it was the structure and anxieties of assessment which determined the experience and enjoyment of independent study.

Indeed, evaluation of both independent study programmes leads to the conclusion that their assessment procedures do not have much to do with their educational goals. There was little attempt to assess the student's individual progress along a route from dependent to independent learning. It would seem reasonable to us that in any scheme of independent study the practice of self-assessment by the student ought to be encouraged. It is true, of course, that at Lancaster students negotiated the form of their assessment during their second year by specifying the areas of study and the mode of assessment, normally a choice between essays and dissertations. But, once that was done, the assessment structure was external to the student, both a goad and a threat, culminating in the situation in which he must be assessed by staff, some of whom (the external examiner at least) would be unknown to him. At NELP, the student made a guided choice of the objectives of his programme, but the decision whether he had succeeded in reaching them was not his. External assessment necessarily came at the end of the period of study. If there is to be a movement by the student from dependence to independence in learning, it would logically need to be paralleled by a movement from external to self-assessment. At the end of the programme of study one of the chief matters for concern ought to be the student's own judgment of his success.

But to assert such ideas—particularly about assessment—is to ignore the political and cultural context both internal and external to English universities and polytechnics. We have already traced the fate of the quasi-Utopian educational ideals of the Lancaster planning group when they attempted to grapple with the decision-making structures of a modern English university, and the difficulties with which the full-time staff of the infant Lancaster school were faced both in terms of the scheme's uncertain survival in a partially hostile environment and of the pressure to be seen to achieve short-term success although with inadequate resources. The relatively easier passage of the NELP proposal was made possible by the overt backing of the polytechnic's directorate, and by its direct association with the slogans of 'relevance' and 'needs' with which NELP has identified itself. This official support meant that the NELP scheme began operation in a form that was much more ambitious and generously endowed with resource, and much less hedged about with compromises and precautions, than was the case at Lancaster. The upshot was the many problems which are documented in Chapter 2 and the various forms of tightening-up which are detailed at the beginning of this chapter. At NELP, and at Lancaster, the reality of independent study has proved far distant from the original ideas of the planning groups in both institutions; the ambiguity of some of those ideas, the varying interpretations of them by participating staff and students, the rivalry and opposition from some sectors of the host institution, curricular and assessment conventions, student needs and problems, all these, and other factors, have constituted the realities of the situation to which the schemes of independent study have had to adapt.

We have not tried to say that the two schemes were identical in conception. Both were radical but the ideological climate in which they were generated was different and they reflected that difference in a number of important ways. The planning group at Lancaster had begun by wanting to transform the university; they had ideals of the academic community and of student-centred teaching and learning to which they wanted to recall their colleagues. For them, it was almost a question of freeing university learning from social contaminations. The ideals of the NELP protagonists were almost opposite. The problem in their perception was that higher education had remained too long unresponsive to social needs. First reform higher education, adapt it to produce generations of graduates with socially necessary skills, then the reform of society could begin.

The NELP scheme drew its justification from certain aspects of a 'mass' model of higher education: near-open entry, a 'value-added' notion of the educational experience ('ability to benefit' as a criterion of selection rather than 'ability to succeed'), academic governance by citizens as well as academics, weakened boundaries between the institution and its environment. The Lancaster programme, on the other hand, drew more on an 'élite' model: restricted entry, a relationship between tutor and student of academic apprenticeship, an emphasis on very high academic standards and accountability to the academic community rather than to the wider non-academic world.

The protagonists of the original schemes at both institutions, one might argue, saw the problems of teaching and learning in higher education in terms that were too simple and which were bound to be modified by experience. But, despite the problems of implementation which this book has emphasized, we have been impressed by the power which those simple ideas have demonstrated in practice. Many students in both schemes revealed without any prompting the involvement and motivation in learning the freedom of independent study had made possible for them. Students were clear that they were on the 'inside' of their studies and that they had an emotional commitment to inquiry which would not have been possible in conventional courses. Staff involved in the schemes often reinforced this view and acknowledged the scope of independent study in allowing students to become critical, and even creative. In Chapter 1 we discussed the concept of independence in study as intrinsic to a notion of a student who had achieved a higher education. In the schemes of independent study at NELP and Lancaster there was, in our view, impressive evidence of this notion in action.

But at what cost? It seems difficult to claim that schemes of independent study, after the models of Lancaster and NELP, could be anything but luxuries for institutions of higher education. Dressel and Thompson (1973) argue that independent study does not necessarily imply a one-to-one staff/student ratio, and the NELP programme has shown that group work in independent study is fruitful (but not without difficulties). The Lancaster scheme, however, is based solely on individual study; the NELP one incorporates a substantial proportion of it. Because of the need to provide staff time and materials for individual schemes of study over a major part of a student's undergraduate career, these courses are bound to cost more—by any measurable criteria—than conventional ones. It is possible to argue that students of independent study have more chance of a 'real' education if they are left to their own devices. In practice, though, this will not do for most students. We have urged the responsibility of an independent study scheme to provide ample tutorial dialogue and supervision for individual students. Significantly Lancaster, in particular, relied heavily on the voluntary, unremunerated, part-time help of staff from all parts of the university. Significantly, too, despite the pressures on university staff to 'publish or perish' in a decade of limited promotion prospects, that voluntary help was normally forthcoming. The simple principle of voluntarism, of a member of staff working with a student on a problem or area of knowledge in which both are interested for its own sake, is another potent feature of schemes of independent study. It is also a unifying feature for an institution of higher education when staff from different sectors and disciplines voluntarily draw together in a common enterprise concerned with students and better learning.

INDEPENDENT STUDY: ITS SUCCESS AND FUTURE DEVELOPMENT
We began this book by saying that the experiments in independent study at NELP

and Lancaster University would, if successful, have important implications for the rest of higher education. Is it possible, on the basis of the evaluatory studies reported in Chapters 2 and 3, to say that they have been successful?

Both schemes have at least been judged successful by formal criteria. The Lancaster School of Independent Studies is no longer an experiment: it has been established as permanent by the university. In approving the full-time DipHE for a five-year period, and in accepting the degree and part-time diploma schemes, the CNAA has acknowledged the permanent value of the NELP School for Independent Study. Graduates and diplomates have been produced in proportions and with a standard of work (despite its unconventional nature) which internal and external examiners find acceptable. In many cases work is acknowledged to be outstanding. Lancaster independent studies graduates are not (as far as is known) unemployed: they have been accepted for research and teacher training and can be found working in the police and prison services, in youth and community work, and in self-employed creative work. NELP diplomates have been accepted on to degree courses or have moved to jobs in, for example, education, social work and screen-printing design. One NELP diplomate, who did his individual work in underwater technology, is now training and safety officer with British Oxygen Sub-ocean Services. Two other early NELP diplomates are self-employed. We do not know, of course, if the independent study students have received an education which is of more long-term use to them in postgraduate life than the one they would have gained from conventional courses because they have all graduated recently. However, it seems reasonable to hypothesize from the interviews conducted in both case studies that most students will have been considerably matured either intellectually or personally, or both, by their experience of independent study.

In a real sense independent study has become established and institutionalized at Lancaster and NELP. No doubt it still has its critics and enemies in both institutions, but there is no prospect of its demise and the university and the polytechnic proudly point to their schools of independent study as symbols of their innovatory initiative. The problems and issues which we have raised in this book do not detract from the value of those initiatives. At the very least, they have laid bare some of the questions about effective student learning which a still expanding system of higher education has yet to confront.

What, then, of the implications of the NELP and Lancaster initiatives for the remainder of higher education? On the basis of what we have written in this book we feel confident in urging that all universities, polytechnics and colleges should develop a school of independent study of a type appropriate to their particular organizational structure and context. Such a body would have a variety of functions. For staff, its arrival would help to foster, or re-fuel, an atmosphere in which undergraduate teaching was perceived to be of primary concern. For a minority of students it would organize programmes of independent study which would constitute the major part of a degree course. But, on the basis of the studies of NELP and Lancaster, we agree with Dressel and Thompson (1973) that all students should have the opportunity and experience of becoming independent learners during a part of their course of undergraduate study. We propose, then, that one unit of all degree and diploma courses should be taken in a school of independent study.

Degree structures vary, of course. Some are subject to the expectations of employers or to the requirements of professional associations. Critics of independent study are quick to point out that independent work may be inappropriate to certain disciplines, particularly the exact sciences—although it is there that the project method has been most developed. It is true that nearly all the students at Lancaster have pursued topics with an arts/social science bias, and that central studies projects at NELP are generally in similar fields. NELP students have shown, however, that independent study can be successfully carried out in engineering, underwater technology, and the teaching of mathematics. The *form* in which independent study is pursued in different fields will differ; and obviously the natural sciences require more extensive preliminary knowledge than other subjects if independent work is to be successfully followed in them. But we do not believe, on present evidence, that there are any areas of knowledge to which independent study is inherently unsuitable. The reluctance of students to pursue independent work which concentrates on scientific fields is probably more a function of academic resistance than of a priori boundaries between appropriate methods of learning in different fields of knowledge.

It could be regarded as a goal of all course development that during one part of any degree or diploma course a student should be able to move outside (and, if he wishes, completely away from) conventional course requirements and in the freer and more open intellectual atmosphere of a school of independent study have the experience of proposing and negotiating a programme of work. This would mean engaging in the process of self-assessment and definition of individual goals. Under his own motivation and determination, the student would seek to fulfil the individual programme to which he had contracted himself. Part of the programme might be carried out in groups by students working on group-defined problems, the groups probably being formed of students from different parts of the institution.

This proposal is more far-reaching than the familiar schemes for projects, for liberal studies in technological courses, or for 'distant minors' or 'Free Ninth Units' in the curricula of the new universities. For it involves transferring the responsibility for the choice of content, methodology of learning, and assessment in one section of his course to the student. We have argued that students differ and that some students find the freedom of independent study much more to their taste and abilities than do others. Student differences would, of course, be reflected in the kinds of independent study programmes for which they opted. Those students who find independent study particularly difficult would at least have the closer structure of the remainder of their course upon which they could fall back.

The question of assessment is (as in all proposals for independent study) a problem. To ensure that the unit of work taken in the school of independent study is given equal weighting and status in all degree or diploma programmes it would have to be assessed—given the norms and expectations inherent in current student culture. What we would expect is that an open attitude to assessment would prevail. Assessment would not be confined to dissertations and essays; it could involve visual, practical and oral presentations; it would seek to combine self, peer and external assessment.

We would also propose that not only should courses be structured so that students might spend part of their time in the school of independent study, but also that the spirit of independent study should permeate the whole of the institution and all sections of undergraduate courses. If our system of higher education is to approach more closely the ideals of educational theorists such as Newman and Rogers—ie if it is to encourage in *all* its students a personal commitment to learning, an internalization of knowledge or the methods of using knowledge—then such a context of learning is indispensable.

We have accepted that the goals of independent study are among the major goals of courses of higher education, and have implied that differences between students mean that students will study more successfully through different intellectual atmospheres, teaching methods and assessment structures. This suggests to us that in all courses students should be presented with a variety of choice from among all possible modes of learning. Course content should not be presented to the student as immutable if it is possible that other areas of content could be studied equally usefully; students should thus be given as much choice as possible in *what is to be learned*. The methodology of learning should not be of a compulsory lecture, laboratory and tutorial format—the techniques of individualized and media learning are developing and there is always the possibility that a student may be more effective simply working on his own; the student could be given as much choice as possible in *how and when he learns*. The assessment structure of a course is liable to define for students the course horizons and the possibilities for learning within it; assessment requirements should be diversified to allow for a choice of course work and/or examinations, dissertation and/or oral presentation, project work or assessment of practical work or experience. At least then the student may perceive the situation as one in which he is allowed to make an independent evaluation of his own strengths and weaknesses, and, by choosing between the modes of assessment, to exercise control over *how his learning is assessed*.

NOTES

[1] The account which follows refers, except where otherwise stated, to the re-submission made in January 1978.

[2] The sub-committee had access to the evaluatory study on which Chapter 3 of this book is based.

John Stephenson   School for Independent Study, North East London
Polytechnic

At the time of writing this postscript, in June 1979, the School for Independent
Study at North East London Polytechnic is preparing for its sixth intake into the
full-time DipHE, the fourth under the revised programme of 1976. Perhaps the most
significant thing to report is just that—we are still thriving.

To date we have recruited over 400 students onto our programmes, the vast
majority of whom have successfully negotiated approved programmes of study. In
the current first year out of an intake of 99 we have 91 students still enrolled. This
represents a substantial improvement on the fall-out rates compared to previous
years, as outlined in the main text. The most important reason for this is greater
clarity amongst staff and students about the nature of independent study. This has
enabled the school to give more confident and accurate information to potential and
actual applicants, to develop clearer understanding of the kinds of students less
likely to benefit, and to present a less ambiguous programme particularly in central
studies.

Current definitions of independent study include the following from (1) *The
Report of the Chairman of the Validating Board,* and (2) *The Development Plan of
the Faculty of Humanities:*

(1) 'We were concerned to clarify the differences between independent study
and individual study. The former relates primarily to the self development
by the student of the ability to formulate problems and test solutions in
unfamiliar situations, and seeks to achieve this by requiring the student
to identify for himself the starting and end points of his studies, his means
of conducting them, and not least important, the criteria on which his
achievement will be judged. Individual study on the other hand describes
a one to one relationship between tutor and student in which the initiation
and control of the purpose and direction of the study may still rest with
the tutor. The two overlap in the DipHE where the student does individual
work by independent study, and this can lead to confusion with other
forms of individual work which are dependent on the tutor (eg language
laboratory work).'

(2) 'The School for Independent Study exists to promote that particular mode
of study. Its four essential features are: firstly, that a student defines for
himself the present stage of his development as well as that which he wishes
to achieve at the end of a specified period of study, and, subject only to
the minimum structure required to ensure comparability of standard where

a final award is sought, he then designs and controls the programme which will enable him to do this; secondly, in following his programme, the student can call on the resources of the whole Polytechnic; thirdly, since his studies are focussed on his own development, they will acquire subject knowledge only to the extent that this is required in solving the problems he has identified; and fourthly, the student's programme will require him to develop and practise those skills he will need in the future. Independent study is characterized by the presence of all four of these ingredients, and it is this essential requirement that distinguishes it from other forms of individual learning that may take place in the polytechnic.'

During this year the school has been in receipt of a minor grant from the Nuffield Foundation to support a follow-up study of our former students. The report on this is not yet complete, but the following comments might be of interest (NB some from students quoted in the main text):

I think I was happy with the course, and feel personally more confident and competent as a result.
> (Student presently taking Degree by Ind. Study)

The DipHE has a lot going for it, but does need a great deal of improvement, especially in the group work area.
> (Student now on 2-year Youth and Community Work course)

Joining the DipHE did me a great service—even though I was unable to complete.
> (Student who withdrew through ill health)

Thank goodness they don't know what sort of course the DipHE at NELP is like. If they did, there would be no chance of any DipHE students from NELP here.
> (Student presently doing third year of BEd course outside NELP—
> together with two other students)

The course enabled me to get a job due to the work completed on my special interest.
> (Geology Technician at University College)

Course still seeking an identity; seems to be more structured each year. Is it in danger of losing its original aim? Enjoyed most of it, though.
> (Presently taking Degree by Ind. Study)

A very good experience . . .
> (Presently taking Degree by Ind. Study)

A very worthwhile experience—and marked a watershed in my personal development.
> (Student now taking Degree in northern college)

Even if I had not gained the diploma, the course itself changed my life and personality; academically, intellectually and emotionally. Well worthwhile.

(Presently on Degree by Ind. Study. No 'O' or 'A' levels)

Needed the Diploma course to find myself.

(Student now doing BSc (Sc) in southern college)

The course was no good to me—mainly because my special interest tutor was not interested. Socially, I enjoyed it very much; made good friends and found it a really good experience.

(Now working as a photo technician)

Experience certainly a help in present position.

(Now lecturing in photography)

I don't regret my two years on the course. Personally they were of great value—but as an academic qualification, I have found it is not yet recognized, though this was to be expected as the course is still new.

(Now clerical assistant in industry)

Still haven't made up my mind—but it got me my meal ticket.

(Now research and organization with White Fish Authority)

An excellent course, allowing for the study of my own chosen area (communication design), eventually to degree level. No other college could have done this for one without 'O' or 'A' levels.

(Currently taking year off to travel)

The school has accumulated three years experience of the Degree by Independent Study, and has awarded its first First Class Honours degree. We are currently negotiating with the CNAA a further approval, and discussion has focused on the criteria for judgment of an Honours degree, the resource support from the rest of the polytechnic, whether written exams should be compulsory and the extent to which there should be a transfer of students from other institutions.

The most significant changes in the school have been administrative. As part of a general review of polytechnic directorate responsibilities the school has been put into a new Faculty of Humanities along with the former Faculty of Arts now named the School of Education and Humanities. This integration into the main body of the institution has obviously removed the isolation of the school but has exposed it more directly to the traditional bureaucratic practices of the rest of the polytechnic, many of which were devised for the needs of traditional courses. It has the further disadvantage of identifying the school with one particular discipline area.

The school is also physically moving into one of the polytechnic's main precincts. This will, no doubt, remove much of the isolation experienced by many students and also will give greater access to learning and recreational resources. One possible danger is that they will identify with some faculties rather than others.

Jane Routh   School of Independent Studies, Lancaster University

Only when one embarks on a new venture does it become evident just how much of our academic life is underpinned by traditions, and quite how much momentum have established practices. The operations of an opposition to an innovation which breaks with established tradition are probably more specific to particular institutions and individuals than are the internal problems of an innovation, from which some generalizations may be possible. These notes focus, therefore, on some internal problems. Many of the early difficulties in Lancaster's School of Independent Studies, which Percy and Ramsden identify, are rooted in the absence of precedents, or in the application of traditional (but inappropriate) models.

The absence of precedents gives rise to anxiety. Percy and Ramsden have described student worry about assessment. Certainly the first group of students had no past papers to consult, but more importantly they had no forerunners in this country on whose advice or traditional wisdom they could lean in respect of study methods, presentation of material, relationships with directors of study and so on. They were creating a new role for themselves—and so were the staff.[1]

This study shows that, in each group, some were more able to cope with the inherent ambiguities than others. The full-time staff had a tightrope to walk, trying to strike a balance between letting the right answers evolve over time in response to actual work and real problems, or formulating guidelines to answer queries which, while stilling disquiet, might restrict or distort development.

There are several instances where the ambiguous demands put on staff and students by the original proposals approved by the senate have been clarified and made more precise, without losing flexibility. One of the most interesting examples is the submissions required from students before they are able to transfer to a major or minor in independent studies. The first group of students had no idea what was expected of them; all were worried about whether they would be able to transfer. A set of written guidelines, culled from documents approved by the senate, and a suggested set of 'contents' were put together, yet caused further anxiety by being too particular: many students could not see how to fit their work into the pattern outlined. Later students had earlier submissions to refer to, and guidelines written to take into account the variety of those submissions. Now a large body of previous submissions exists, as well as a set of 'mock' submissions, written by the staff to show particular weaknesses and strengths (which had the not entirely incidental, but salutory, effect of teaching the staff who wrote them just what a difficult task had been set to students). No amount of advice from staff in those first years could have provided the reassurance that this library does.

Such is the momentum of established practices that there are some areas where they are all too easily imported without any thought for their real purpose—perhaps most notably in assessment and in administration. The first graduates all opted to have their work assessed by dissertations—partly, of course, as a reaction against the tradition of final examination papers. But the prevalence of dissertations was also a failure of imagination on the part of both students and staff—and showed apprehension about risks. There were sufficient unknown quantities without adding to them the sort of proposals which the 1979 and 1980 graduates are putting forward —among them an exhibition, an unseen examination paper, practical work in sculpture, a short story, and reports on participant observation. A cautious but steady development of alternative patterns has encouraged present students to propose appropriate alternative assessments. When three 'blind' markers concur, staff gain confidence in the feasibility of assessing different types of work.

Similarly, administrative routines applicable elsewhere on campus were early imported into the school. After all, it was a place for learning in new ways, and there was enough to do in thinking this through, without questioning every administrative procedure. Yet the administrative load in such a school is very high indeed: every student has his own programme of work, timetable, resources, directors of study as well as some regular, taught courses. Initially the administration was organized around specific jobs, or around year groups, which increased the perception of such tasks as routine (and boring), since they are divorced from the school's teaching role.

This, as well as a surprising number of the difficulties which have been identified in this book, has been overcome by a single development—the introduction of 'contact groups'. It was recognized at the outset that students working on individual projects were not benefiting from discussions with their peers, but it took some time to restore this level of debate. (In the academic year 1975/6 the university's economies were extremely damaging to the school: with only one full-time member of staff, the school became de facto an administrative unit in students' eyes. Not unnaturally, later generations resisted the re-introduction of seminars, or 'extra work'.)

Early seminars for all students spanned too great a range of interests for students to grant them much importance, and were replaced by small groups, each with a full-time member of staff whose own academic expertise related to the students' work. These contact groups have become the basis of student participation in the school, *and* the basis on which the administrative work is now organized. Each member of staff undertakes the administrative tasks for his or her group of students, from advising on initial ideas to discussing career options. By being student-centred rather than system-centred, the administrative work is seen as less of a chore, and appreciated more for its proper function. The administrative officer checks on the administration throughout, but he himself (having an academic background) takes a contact group.

The spread of expertise between the four full-time members of staff is such that it is possible to divide students into four main academic groupings (arts; philosophy and religious studies; politics and sociology; history.) General seminars in each contact group on topics like source material are pertinent to the work of all in the group, and by splitting into two or three subsidiary meetings, seminar groups are able to discuss common themes or to make relevant contributions to problems encountered by one member of the group in his or her work.

Not only have the contact groups re-introduced peer group contact, but they have also alleviated a range of other difficulties. All students have regular contact, at an academic as well as an administrative level, with a member of the academic staff other than their director of studies. New points of view are brought to students' attention. Careful monitoring and early diagnosis of problems are much easier, as a member of the school's staff has a full picture of the students' progress.

An important result of contact groups for students is that the basis of student representation has shifted and become more effective. The six student representatives on the Committee for Independent Studies have a strong voice, but it was not a coherent one while elections were held among the group at large and students reported back to a general assembly, which never had time to deal with the day-to-day running of the school. While the assembly still exists as a forum for policy-making, the contact groups are now the constituencies for the student representatives, who meet with the full-time staff on a frequent and regular basis to work out the minutiae of school business. Contact groups have thus greatly strengthened student involvement with the school, academically, socially, and politically.

Some of the problems have, then, been eased, but more developments are needed. The school is pressing for the use of half-time staff, lending its own people out to departments, and bringing in—for one, two or three-year periods—teaching staff from other departments who can contribute to and gain from its work. Where economies render career patterns inflexible, this type of opportunity is to be welcomed in universities.

Students are now proposing different forms of assessment, but we still need to give the role of assessment in independent studies more thought. Our students, when asked, have expressed unease at the thought of self-assessment, yet at the request of the Committee for Independent Studies, several have now introduced timetabling and staggered deadlines into their work. A certain amount of conflict between students' personal development and the formal requirements of a university Honours degree will probably always be with us, but it is noteworthy that increasingly our board of examiners has had before it not just marks, but long and careful reports on the work from external examiners and 'blind' internal markers and from the director of study on the work and the student's development. Within the limits of confidentiality required by the university, these provide a most important final feedback to the student on his or her work.

74

If there is any overall pattern to be detected in the development of the school over the last seven years, it is a movement away from what has been described earlier as 'careful academic pragmatism' back towards the optimistic philosophy of the original planning group. To a certain extent this is forcing false dichotomies, because the school continued to receive the generous voluntary help of many members of the planning group as directors of study and as members of the Committee for Independent Studies. But the school certainly has—in spite of the continuing recalcitrant individualism of some independent members—a greater unity of purpose, and a more articulate set of shared assumptions about the nature and value of independent development than it has had at some times before.

And again, if it is not forcing false dichotomies too far, the school's work is closer to that undertaken at NELP than it has been before: for there the movement has, if anything, been the other way round—a little less philosophy, a little more pragmatism.

July 1979

[1]Nor were precedents really available in North America: a study visit in 1973 to the United States and Canada found the available models not relevant to Lancaster's work. Most independent study departments were administrative units run on a 'supermarket' basis to facilitate dissertation options.

REFERENCES

ADDERLEY, K. et al. (1975) *Project Methods in Higher Education.* London: SRHE.

ALLEN B. and DRAPER, M. (1975) *The DipHE.* Unpublished report to staff.

AYDELOTTE, F. (1924) Honors courses in American colleges and universities. *Bulletin of the National Research Council,* 7, Part 4 (40) 9-18.

AYDELOTTE, F. (1944) *Breaking the Academic Lock Step.* New York: Harper and Row.

BECKER, H. S. (1952) Social class variations in the teacher-pupil relationship. *Journal of Educational Sociology,* 25, 451-465.

BERNSTEIN, B. B. (1971) On the classification and framing of educational knowledge. In Young, M.F.D. (ed.) *Knowledge and Control.* London: Collier Macmillan.

BONTHIUS, R. H. et al. (1957) *The Independent Study Program in the United States.* New York: Columbia University Press.

BOUD, D. and BRIDGE, W. (1974) Keller plan: a case study in individualized learning. Paper given to Nuffield Group Seminar for Research and Innovation in Higher Education on Independence in Learning, 25-28 February 1974. In NUFFIELD 1975.

BRENNAN, J. L. and PERCY, K. A. (1977) What do students want? An analysis of staff and student perceptions in British higher education. In Bonboir, A. (ed.). *Instructional design in higher education.* European Association for Research and Development in Higher Education, 1, 125-152.

BRICK, M. and McGRATH, E. J. (1969) *Innovation in Liberal Arts Colleges.* New York: Teachers College Press.

BRIDGE, W. and ELTON, L. (1977) *Individual Study in Undergraduate Science.* London: Heinemann.

BROSAN, G. S. (1971a) A self-limited function. In Brosan, G. S., Carter C., Layard, R., Venables, P., and Williams, G. *Patterns and Policies in Higher Education.* Harmondsworth: Penguin.

BROSAN, G. S. (1971b) A polytechnic philosophy. In Brosan, G. S., et al. *Patterns and Policies in Higher Education.* Harmondsworth: Penguin.

BURGESS, T. (1977) *Education after School.* Harmondsworth: Penguin.

DEPARTMENT OF EDUCATION AND SCIENCE (1972) *Education: A Framework for Expansion.* Cmnd. 5174, London: HMSO.

DEWEY, J. (1916) *Democracy and Education.* New York: Macmillan.

DRESSEL, P. L. and DeLISLE, F. H. (1969) *Undergraduate Curriculum Trends.* Washington: American Council on Education.

DRESSEL, P. L. and THOMPSON, M. M. (1973) *Independent Study.* San Francisco: Jossey-Bass.

EATON, D. (1976) Preliminary report on the DipHE. In NELP 1976.

ENTWISTLE, N. J. and PERCY, K. A. (1971) Educational objectives and student performance within the binary system. In *Research into Higher Education 1970.* London: SRHE.

ENTWISTLE, N. J. and PERCY, K. A. (1974) Critical thinking or conformity? An investigation of the aims and outcomes of higher education. In *Research into Higher Education 1973.* London: SRHE.

ENTWISTLE, N. J. and WILSON, D. (1977) *Degrees of Excellence: The Academic Achievement Game.* London: Hodder and Stoughton.

FULTON, J. (1966) The University of Sussex. In Ross, M. G. (ed.) *New Universities in the Modern World.* London: Macmillan.

JAMES, E. (1972) *Teacher Education and Training.* Report of a committee under the chairmanship of Lord James of Rusholme. London: HMSO.

KARABEL, J. and HALSEY, A. H. (1977) *Power and Ideology in Education.* New York: OUP.

LANCASTER UNIVERSITY SENATE (1977) *Report of the Independent Studies Review Committee.*

LEWIN, J. S. J. (1976) *Independent Studies at the University of Lancaster* Unpublished M.A. dissertation, University of Lancaster.

LEWIS, H. A. (1978) A teacher's reflections on autonomy. In *Studies in Higher Education,* 3, (2), 149–159.

LUKES, J. R. (1967) The binary policy: a critical study. *Universities Quarterly,* December 1967, 6–46.

MASLOW, A. H. (1973) *The Farther Reaches of Human Nature.* Harmondsworth: Penguin.

NELP (1973) *Diploma of Higher Education: A Proposal.* Report of a working party set up by the Director of the North East London Polytechnic, March 1973.

NELP (1975) *Prospectus: School for Independent Study.*

NELP (1976) *Full-time Diploma of Higher Education.* Report to CNAA, September 1976.

NELP (1977) *Diploma of Higher Education* (Prospectus).

NELP (1978) *Application for Renewal of Approval: Degree by Independent Study.*

NELP (nd) *Faculty of Human Sciences Development Committee: Consideration of submission of proposal to the CNAA for a BA by independent studies.*

NEWMAN, J. H. (1852) *On the Scope and Nature of University Education.* London: Dent.

NUFFIELD GROUP (1975) *Towards Independence in Learning: Selected Papers.* London: Nuffield Foundation.

POPPER, K. R. (1959) *The Logic of Scientific Discovery.* London: Hutchinson.

RAMSDEN, P. (1975) *The DipHE: A report.* Unpublished report to staff, July 1975.

ROBINSON, E. E. (1968) *The New Polytechnics.* Harmondsworth: Penguin.

ROGERS, C. R. (1969) *Freedom to Learn.* Columbus, Ohio: Merrill.

STARTUP, R. (1972) How students see the role of university lecturer. *Sociology,* 6, 237–254.

TROW, M. (1972) Binary dilemmas—an American view. In Burgess, T. (ed.) *The Shape of Higher Education.* London: Cornmarket Press.

UMSTATTD, J. G. (1935) The prevalence and practice of independent study. *Journal of Higher Education,* 6, 364–376.

YOUNG, M. F. D. (1971) An approach to the study of curricula as socially organized knowledge. In Young, M. F. D. (ed.) *Knowledge and Control.* London: Collier Macmillan.

INDEX